Author Welcome: Good luck with your study of the federal and state governments. *Our Federal Constitution, Our Indiana Constitution* worktext is designed to help study the most important document ever written, principles of our democracy, and the foundation of our government. A practical study of government will make you a better citizen and help to improve the government under which we all live. To answer the "Questions" section in each unit, read the unit first. This reading will increase your understanding of the material and improve your quizzes and the constitution test performance. Your school has joined many others in making this a critical component of the civics curriculum..
— *Alex J. Schmidt*

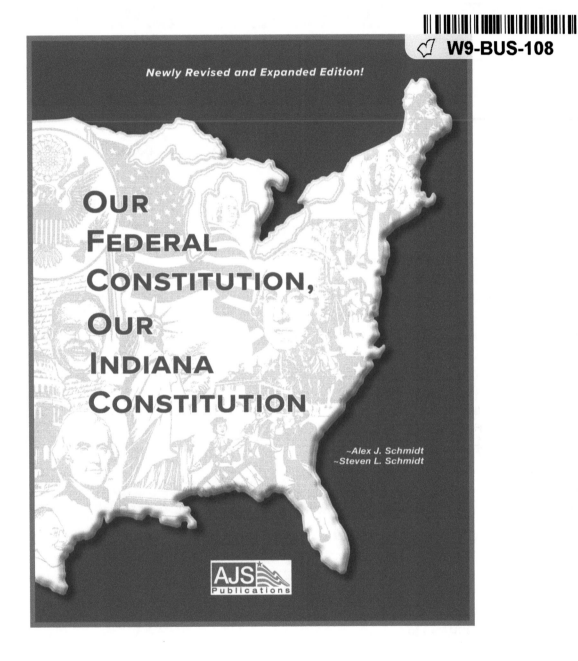

Newly Revised and Expanded Edition!

OUR FEDERAL CONSTITUTION, OUR INDIANA CONSTITUTION

~Alex J. Schmidt
~Steven L. Schmidt

AJS Publications

Published by
AJS Publications, Inc.
2305 Mills Pond Road, Crystal Lake, IL 60014
Orders accepted by contacting us below:
Phone: (847) 526-5027, Fax: (847) 487-5229
email: info@ajspublications.com
www.ajspublications.com
ISBN 978-1-892291-10-3 DMTN-POD
©2022, Alex J. Schmidt, Steven L. Schmidt

FEDERAL SECTION

INDIANA SECTION

Welcome Students, to *Our Federal Constitution, Our Indiana Constitution*
Purpose of this Text:

Our Federal Constitution, Our Indiana Constitution worktext is designed to help study the most significant document ever written, principles of our democracy, and the foundation of our government. It is also written to prepare for a final review on those subjects and to help pass that examination.

Goals of This Text

There are two primary goals of this text: **1.** To make you a better citizen of this country through basic knowledge of the Constitution and government of the United States. **2.** To help pass the required state and federal constitutions curriculum or test. This worktext is formatted and written to ensure these goals are met.

Features That Aid in Your Learning

1. Answer all lesson questions. At the end of each unit in this book, there are a series of questions about that lesson. Always be sure to fill in all answers and verify that they are correct. Final constitution test questions come from these pages. The teacher can expand on topics covered in the various units and will assist in any difficult concepts.

2. Read the federal and state outlines. The federal section outline on Pages 47-48 and state outline on Pages 77-78 provides a quick refresher of the fundamental principals and information discussed in this worktext.

3. Answer the review questions. The questions on Pages 49-50 of the federal section and Pages 79 in the state section help confirm your knowledge of the units covered in this worktext. Answering these questions will aid in your success in this area of study.

4. Complete the self-tests. At the end of the federal section on Pages 50-52 and at the end of the state section on Pages 80-81, you will find self-tests on the constitutions and governments. Included are a variety of questions from all of the units. These test questions are similar to the questions on the final exam. The correct answers are at the bottom of the page, check your work.

5. Create practice quizzes to help review for tests. Use questions from the units in the book, from the self-tests, and from the review questions and outlines, or just make up your own. You could trade practice quizzes with other students.

The signing of the Constitution, September 17, 1787.

The early colonists came to America to find freedom, but had to face many dangers. They became very independent and self-sufficient. At first, England paid little attention to the colonists in America, and the colonists were not strictly controlled by English law and government.

However, after the colonies grew and became essential trade centers, the British imposed restrictions and trade regulations on them. Some of these restrictions put England in a favorable position concerning trade with the colonies. The colonies objected vigorously.

The colonists also objected to the quartering of soldiers, taxation without representation in Parliament, and lack of true self-government, among other issues.

People soon banded together and, at the urging of patriotic groups like the *Sons of Liberty*, refused to buy English goods.

Patrick Henry

Incidents like the *Boston Tea Party* in 1773 added fuel to the revolution. The Boston Tea Party occurred when patriots, disguised as Indians, threw tons of tea into Boston Harbor because the colonists did not like tax policies of the British. When the British punished the Bostonians, all the colonists were inflamed. Conditions grew worse and, a year after the Boston Tea Party, Patrick Henry shouted:

"The next gale that sweeps from the north will bring to our ears the clash of resounding arms! Our brethren are already in the field! Why stand we here idle? What is it that gentlemen wish? What would they have? Is life so dear, or peace so sweet, as to be purchased at the price of chains and slavery? Forbid it, Almighty God! I know not what course others may take; but as for me, give me liberty, or give me death!"

Henry's speech became one of the best-known pre-revolutionary speeches.

First Continental Congress

Colonial leaders decided to call a meeting to discuss how to win their rights. They were more interested in fair treatment than in independence. The *First Continental Congress* met at Carpenters' Hall in Philadelphia, Pennsylvania, in 1774, with delegates from 12 of the 13 colonies. Georgia did not send representatives but agreed to support any plans made at the meeting. The delegates sent their complaints to the king, but British colonial policy did not change. Although they wanted their rights, delegates did not dream they would soon have the responsibility of conducting a war. The colonial leaders also

Carpenters' Hall

imposed an *embargo* (agreement prohibiting trade) on British trade and goods.

Second Continental Congress

The First Continental Congress adjourned in late October 1774 but agreed to convene the following May. By then the *American Revolution* had begun. In the spring of 1775, British soldiers were sent to Lexington, Massachusetts, to seize the guns and ammunition of the colonists and arrest colonial leaders Samuel Adams and John Hancock. It was Paul Revere who warned the Minutemen to meet British soldiers at Lexington, where an unidentified shot started the war.

The *Second Continental Congress* met a few weeks later in May 1775, again in Philadelphia. Many of the same 56 delegates who attended the first meeting were in attendance, including one from each of the 13 colonies. These delegates had first come hoping for peace, but soon, more and more leaders called for complete separation from Great Britain.

Many critical actions were discussed and decided. The Second Continental Congress assumed the powers of a central government. An army and a navy were organized, and money was issued. General George Washington was chosen to lead the army. The Second Continental Congress became the nation's first government and continued to meet until the Articles of Confederation took effect in 1781.

Six years after the fighting began in Lexington, the British surrendered to General Washington at Yorktown, Virginia. The Americans had won their fight for independence.

QUESTIONS

TRUE OR FALSE? Write a *T* or *F* in the space provided.

____ 1. The only objection the colonists had toward British rule concerned trade regulations.

____ 2. When the First Continental Congress met, the members wanted to declare war against England.

____ 3. Patrick Henry did not want to see the war begin.

____ 4. The Sons of Liberty supported the colonists' cause.

____ 5. The English colonists were closely governed from the time of the earliest settlements.

____ 6. The Boston Tea Party occurred because of a tax dispute.

____ 7. Samuel Adams and John Hancock were colonial leaders.

____ 8. Patrick Henry said, "Give me liberty, or give me death!"

____ 9. The First Continental Congress met in 1774.

____ 10. Each of the 13 colonies had a representative at the Second Continental Congress.

____ 11. George Washington led the American Army in the Revolution.

____ 12. The British won the American Revolution.

From Revolution to Independence

On June 7, 1776, more than a year after the Revolution began, Richard Henry Lee of Virginia introduced this resolution to the Second Continental Congress:

"That these United Colonies are, and of right ought to be, free and independent States, that they are absolved from all allegiance to the British Crown, and that all political connection between them and the State of Great Britain is, and ought to be, totally dissolved."

The resolution proposed independence for the American colonies. Following a spirited debate, the delegates agreed to the *Lee Resolution* on July 2. A couple of days later, on July 4, 1776, the Declaration of Independence was adopted. As a result, this date is celebrated as *Independence Day*. It gave various reasons why the colonists wanted to separate from England and announced the existence of a new nation.

The Declaration was written by Thomas Jefferson and a committee from the Second Continental Congress. While the words were mostly Thomas Jefferson's, the ideas were centuries old. The Declaration can be divided into three parts: **(1)** a statement of principle concerning the rights of a man and why a revolution was necessary, **(2)** a list of specific grievances against England's King George III, and **(3)** a formal claim of independence. The most important part of the Declaration comes in its second paragraph:

Thomas Jefferson

"We hold these truths to be self-evident, that all men are created equal, that they are endowed by their Creator with certain unalienable Rights, that among these are Life, Liberty and the pursuit of Happiness. That to secure these rights, Governments are instituted among Men, deriving their just powers from the consent of the governed."

The Declaration is Read to the Public

On July 8, 1776, church bells were rung throughout Philadelphia to call the people to the first public reading of the Declaration. For the safety of the delegates, their names were not made public for six months. When they were revealed, many were seized by the British and thrown into prison, and their homes were burned. This small group had risked their lives for liberty.

Nearly a month would pass before the document was signed. New York's officials did not officially give their support until July 9. Also, it took two weeks for the Declaration to be "engrossed" or the process of writing on parchment paper. Most of the delegates signed on August 2, but several signed on a later date, along with two representatives never signing at all.

Today, in Philadelphia, there stands a tablet that marks the place where Thomas Jefferson wrote the Declaration. After Congress had adopted the Declaration, John Dunlap printed copies of it. These prints are now called *Dunlap Broadsides*. Twenty-four copies are known to exist, two of which are in the Library of Congress. The original copy was exhibited for many years until light and air threatened its existence. In 1921, it was transferred to the care of the Library of Congress. In 1952, it was placed in the National Archives building in Washington, D.C. You may see it there, and you also may visit the meeting place of the Second Continental Congress in Philadelphia.

The important fact is not that the Americans had declared themselves independent, but that they had set down certain principles and beliefs that were new to governments: all men are created equal; all men have rights; and governments are subject to the will of the people.

The Declaration of Independence is not a constitution or form of government. It served to set up principles for a new government. Such beliefs were used in writing the United States Constitution.

QUESTIONS

MULTIPLE CHOICE: Circle the letter of the correct answer.

1. Which of the following is NOT an unalienable right of the Declaration?
   a. life
   b. liberty
   c. education
   d. pursuit of happiness

2. The Declaration was written by:
   a. Thomas Jefferson
   b. George Washington
   c. Alexander Hamilton
   d. John Adams

3. The Declaration was authorized by the:
   a. Second Continental Congress
   b. First Continental Congress
   c. British King
   d. New England Confederation

4. The Declaration was signed and adopted in:
   a. 1727   b. 1775   c. 1776   d. 1876

5. The Declaration of Independence included:
   a. statements concerning the rights of individuals
   b. a list of specific grievances against England
   c. a formal claim of independence from England
   d. all of the above

TRUE OR FALSE? Write a *T* or *F* in the space provided.

____ 1. The Declaration was written to start the American Revolution.

____ 2. The Second Continental Congress had the task of carrying out the American Revolution.

____ 3. The Declaration of Independence is not a constitution.

____ 4. The Declaration was written in Washington, D.C.

____ 5. The principles of the Declaration of Independence were used in writing the U.S. Constitution.

____ 6. The Declaration of Independence was signed after the U.S. Constitution was written.

____ 7. Richard Henry Lee wrote a resolution that would allow England more authority over the colonists.

____ 8. A delegate is a person that represents others, speaking, and acting on their behalf.

In the months after the Declaration of Independence was signed, Congress wanted to continue to unite the former colonies. The first attempt at a national or federal government came in the form of the *Articles of Confederation*. The Articles, adopted by the Second Continental Congress in 1777, were not ratified by all the states until 1781.

The Articles of Confederation acted as the first constitution of the United States. The Articles were in use until the Constitution was signed in 1787. The Articles were weak because the colonists were reluctant to give much power to a central government. The colonies feared that a new central government might be no better than the English king had been. The states themselves had governments at this time, most with state constitutions.

When it became necessary to have a *national* or *federal government* for conducting the Revolutionary War, the states made the government weak. The Articles were so weak that the government could not even pay its bills. It did have limited powers to make war or peace, but other powers were lacking. Robert Morris, known as the *Financier of the Revolution*, stated that getting money from the states was like "preaching to the dead." To raise money, the central government could only ask the states for funds; it could not tax.

Robert Morris

At the end of the Revolutionary War, the American government was in severe financial trouble. Soldiers who had served without pay were granted western land certificates instead of money, but most had to sell their certificates for cash. Farmers with large debts rebelled against the courts that were taking away their farms. An example of such a rebellion was the *Shays' Rebellion* by farmers in Massachusetts. Jails were crowded with debtors. States were taxing each other harmfully and arguing about land claims to the West. Tariff laws were needed for business and industry. Prices soared, and credit disappeared. It became increasingly evident that the only solution was a stronger central government.

Weaknesses of the Articles

Listed below are weaknesses identified by the colonists:

- No national courts, only state courts.
- No power to tax.
- No real power to regulate commerce.
- All changes in the Articles had to be approved by all of the states.
- All important laws had to be approved by nine states.
- No real president, only a president of Congress who was like a chairman.

Morris, who became the superintendent of finance under the Articles, forged a solution by stabilizing the value of paper money. His plan to fund the national debt and deposit federal money in a private bank helps save the United States from financial catastrophe.

Civil Rights and the Articles

Civil rights are those that are considered to be unquestionable, deserved by all people under all circumstances, especially without regard to race, creed, color, or gender. These personal rights are guaranteed and protected by the Constitution.

The fight for civil rights didn't wait until the 1950s to happen. Some started as early as the Articles of Confederation! Paul Cuffee was a free black from Massachusetts. When he discovered he did not have the same property rights as whites, he refused to pay his taxes and was jailed. Cuffee later became a successful trader with a fleet of ships and continued to fight for equal rights throughout his lifetime.

QUESTIONS

*MATCH THE STATEMENT IN **SECTION A** WITH THE TERM IN **SECTION B**.*

A

____ 1. Started by farmers in Massachusetts who were losing their farms.

____ 2. Form of government during the American Revolution.

____ 3. Had to approve important acts under the Articles.

____ 4. Fear of this was in the minds of many American colonists in the 1780s.

____ 5. This power was lacking in the Articles of Confederation.

B

a. states   b. Shays' Rebellion   c. taxation
d. strong central government e. Articles of Confederation

TRUE OR FALSE? Write a *T* or *F* in the space provided.

____ 1. The Articles of Confederation acted as the first U.S. Constitution.

____ 2. The Articles were weak because of the fear of a strong central government.

____ 3. Shays' Rebellion was carried out to support a weak central government.

____ 4. The Declaration of Independence was signed before the Articles of Confederation were written.

____ 5. The Articles were drawn up by the Second Continental Congress.

____ 6. Freedom from discrimination is considered an example of a civil right.

SHORT ANSWER

Explain what Morris meant by his statement "preaching to the dead." _____
_____
_____

In 1786, at Annapolis, Maryland, a meeting was held to discuss commerce problems. Five states attended. During the discussions, a future meeting was proposed. The hope was expressed that all states would participate. This future meeting, or convention, would be held in Philadelphia for the purpose of correcting faults in the Articles of Confederation. As we will learn, the outcome was much larger. They created the *Constitution of the United States*.

The Delegates

The convention began its work in May of 1787 and finished in September of the same year. More than 70 men had been chosen as *delegates* by the various states, but only 55 attended in Philadelphia. A delegate is a person sent to a meeting or conference to represent the interests of the state. The average attendance each day was approximately 30 members. Rhode Island, distrustful of a powerful federal government, was the only one of the 13 original states to refuse to send delegates to the Constitutional Convention.

The men who attended the convention were of remarkable ability. From Virginia came George Washington, Edmond Randolph, and James Madison. New York sent Alexander Hamilton. Pennsylvania sent Benjamin Franklin, Gouverneur Morris, and James Wilson. From New Jersey were William Livingston and William Peterson. Other key delegates were: Elbridge Gerry and Rufus King, Massachusetts; Oliver Ellsworth and Roger Sherman, Connecticut; John Dickinson, Delaware; and John Rutledge and Charles C. Pickney from South Carolina.

The delegates were men of wealth and prestige. Many of them had served in the Revolutionary War and the First and Second Continental Congresses. Many had served in their state governments. Eight had been signers of the Declaration of Independence. Two would become presidents of the United States, and one would become vice president. Eighteen would become senators, and eight would become representatives.

The average age of the men attending the convention was 42, yet many were in their 30s. Ben Franklin was the oldest at 81. Not all of the leaders of the colonies consented to attend, however. Patrick Henry "smelt a rat" and would not attend. Later, he would become a bitter foe of the Constitution, accepting it only after the addition of the Bill of Rights. Samuel Adams and John Hancock also refused to attend, and Thomas Jefferson and Thomas Paine were in Europe.

Independence Hall is the location where both the Declaration and Constitution were debated and adopted.

The Convention at Work

The delegates met in Philadelphia in Independence Hall. Dirt had been spread on the cobblestone street outside the hall, so noise from passing carriages would not disturb the meeting. George Washington was selected as president of the convention. Although the official purpose of the convention was to improve the Articles of Confederation, a decision was quickly reached to replace the Articles with a new constitution. The delegates agreed on an early resolution:

> *"Resolved...that a national government ought to be established consisting of a Supreme, Legislative, Judiciary, and Executive."*

The delegates often disagreed on proposals. However, they all agreed that the new government had to be strong enough to rule the entire nation. Lessons learned under the Articles were put into practice, and this new and improved constitution would:

1. make the Constitution the highest authority in the land;
2. provide for an effective central government;
3. protect the rights of the people by setting limits on governmental authority.

The third objective was the most difficult — creating a constitution that would achieve a balance between liberty and authority.

Slavery and the Constitution

How could a country like the United States, so interested in freedom, not outlaw slavery in 1781? Many northern states had outlawed slavery. But the delegates at the Constitutional Convention knew southern states would never accept the Constitution if it interfered with slavery. So to create the new government, the delegates did not outlaw slavery. Instead, they left the problem for another day and another war. Unfortunately, even with the other freedoms guaranteed by the Bill of Rights, slavery was not outlawed, but slavery's days were numbered.

Who was missing from the Convention?

Who was missing from the Constitutional Convention? No women, Black people, Native Americans, or White people of modest or poor means attended the Constitutional Convention. This was not surprising since most of the above groups could not even vote then.

QUESTIONS

TRUE OR FALSE? Write a *T* or *F* in the space provided.

____ 1. The Constitutional Convention was held in Philadelphia in 1787.

____ 2. The Annapolis Convention did not aid in the process of getting a new constitution written.

____ 3. There were 13 delegates to the convention.

____ 4. George Washington was the president of the Constitutional Convention.

____ 5. The official purpose of the Constitutional Convention was to write the Bill of Rights.

____ 6. The convention at Annapolis came before the Constitutional Convention.

____ 7. The building where the convention met is called Independence Hall.

____ 8. The average age of the men attending the convention was 65.

Problems and Compromises

The first significant difficulty that the convention had to face was the struggle for power between the small states and the large states. The *Virginia Plan*, submitted by James Madison, proposed two houses of Congress based on population. In that way, the large states would control the government. Also, these houses would appoint other necessary government officers, and, therefore, the large states would be in control of the entire government.

On the other hand, the small states proposed the *New Jersey Plan*, which would have made one house of Congress. This was also known as the *Small State Plan* and was presented at the Philadelphia Convention by William Paterson. All the states would be represented equally regardless of size. Other provisions would have made the new Constitution much like the Articles of Confederation.

A compromise was reached (sometimes referred to as the *Great* or *Connecticut Compromise*). The new government would have two houses of Congress. In the House of Representatives, each state would be represented according to population, satisfying the large states. In the Senate, each state would be represented equally, satisfying the small states.

Other compromises regarded the slave trade, the term of the president, voting qualifications, and whether or not to count slaves as people when deciding how many representatives the state would get in the House of Representatives. The *Three-Fifths Compromise* decided that three-fifths of the slaves would count toward representation.

Delegate Distrust of the People

We can see that the delegates distrusted the people in many ways. For example, they decided that the president should be elected by *electors* from the states and not by the people as a whole. This created the *Electoral College,* which assigned electors to each state. Each state received as many electors as its total of senators and representatives in Congress. Later in U.S. history, these electors in the Electoral College would be required to vote for the presidential candidate that won the popular vote in their state. You will learn more about the Electoral College on Page 32.

What is the *popular vote*? It simply means the vote of the people. So when a candidate in your state wins the popular vote, he or she simply won more votes of the people than his or her opponent. A vote by only certain people (like a vote in the U.S. House of Representatives, for example) is not a direct vote of the people, and therefore, not the popular vote.

Another distrust of the people can be seen in the election of United States senators. The Constitutional Convention decided that senators would be elected by state legislators, not the people themselves. However, later, the 17th Amendment to the Constitution changed that. The people in the states now elect their senators.

The lack of trust of the common people was due partly to there being very few representatives of the common man at the Constitutional Convention. Forty of the 55 delegates were wealthy enough to have loaned money to the government, 15 were slaveholders, and 14 held western land. None were small farmers or working men. And the champions of the common man, including Jefferson and Henry, were not present.

Many of the democratic features we know in our government today an have evolved since the Constitutional Convention. The writers of the Constitution may have had some distrust of democracy. However, they wrote a document that was flexible enough to provide the basis for orderly change. Most of these changes have made our country more democratic as the years have passed. If you need some examples of this new democracy, imagine how many more people today can vote, run for office, obtain an education, and exercise individual rights.

This is also the time for students to have a definition of *democracy*. Democracy is simply government by the people, exercised either directly or through elected representatives.

The 13 Colonies

These 13 colonies won their freedom in the Revolutionary War; however, they needed the Constitution to unite the states as one nation.

Ratification

The convention adjourned on September 17, 1787, with 39 of the 55 delegates signing the new document. The fight for ratification has begun. The Constitution would take effect once it was approved by nine of the thirteen state Legislatures.

The battle was a bitter one. The Federalists supported the Constitution. Leading Federalists Hamilton, Jay, and Madison published the *Federalist Papers*. These papers were essential in convincing people that the Constitution was of value. The *Anti- Federalists* fought against the Constitution but were not successful.

On June 21, 1788, the Constitution took effect when New Hampshire became the ninth state to ratify it. The remaining four states joined by 1790. The Federalists and Anti-Federalists continued their battle over the Constitution and became two separate political forces under the new government.

On January 7, 1789, the United States, having recently adopted its Constitution, held its first presidential election. Only white men who owned property voted. They choose electors who, in turn, voted for the candidates. As it did in 1789, the United States still uses the Electoral College system established by the U.S. Constitution.

Our First President

As expected, George Washington won the election and was sworn into office on April 30, 1789, as the first president of the United States and the "Father of Our Country." Washington was a Virginia landowner who had led the patriotic forces in the war against the British. His accomplishments matched his popularity.

Washington was a delegate to both Continental Congresses. He was unanimously named both as commander-in-chief of the Continental Army during the Revolutionary War and as president of the Constitutional Convention that drafted the Constitution.

George Washington

Washington finished first with 69 votes, followed by his fellow Federalist John Adams of Massachusetts, whose 34 votes propelled him into the vice presidency. (Before the ratification of the 12th Amendment in 1804, the candidate who received the most electoral votes became president while the runner-up became vice president.)

Citizenship and Becoming President

The members of the Constitutional Convention envisioned a president born in the good, old United States of America. In Article 2, Section 1, they wrote that "No person except a natural-born citizen... shall be eligible to the office of president." The convention delegates did not want to take the chance of a foreign country sending someone to run for our highest political office. Immigrants can become citizens, thus becoming *naturalized* citizens. But naturalized citizens cannot become president; only natural-born citizens are eligible.

QUESTIONS

TRUE OR FALSE? Write a *T* or *F* in the space provided.

____ 1. Six states had to approve the Constitution before it was effective.

____ 2. The Federalists were against the Constitution.

____ 3. The authors of the Constitution wrote a document that was easily adapted to change.

____ 4. The small states wanted each state to have the same number of representatives.

____ 5. The Constitutional Convention adopted the Virginia Plan.

____ 6. Fortunately, the Constitution outlawed slavery.

____ 7. The Electoral College showed that the Constitutional Convention trusted the people.

____ 8. The New Jersey Plan suggested only one house of Congress.

____ 9. The New Jersey Plan favored the small states and the Virginia Plan favored the large states.

____ 10. Each state gets the same number of votes in the Electoral College.

____ 11. Article 2 of the U.S. Constitution includes a provision that only "natural-born" citizens are eligible to become president.

____ 12. Immigrants can become citizens.

MATCH THE PERSON TO THE STATEMENT. Write the letter of the statement that matches the person.

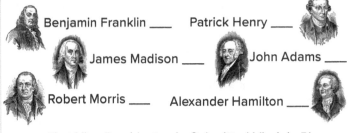

Benjamin Franklin ____   Patrick Henry ____

James Madison ____   John Adams ____

Robert Morris ____   Alexander Hamilton ____

a. First Vice President   **b.** Submitted Virginia Plan

c. NY Delegate & Federalist   **d.** Financier of the Revolution

e. "Smelt a Rat"   **f.** Oldest Delegate at Convention

SHORT ANSWER / FILL IN THE BLANKS

1. Write a definition of democracy. _____
_____
_____

2. Number of the amendment that changed the way we elect U.S. senators. _____

3. Name three of the original 13 colonies. _____
_____

4. The Constitutional Convention adjourned on what date?_____.

5. How many states had to ratify the Constitution before it went into effect? _____

"I will tell you now what I do not like. (There is no) bill of rights, providing . . . what the people are entitled to against every government on earth." —— Thomas Jefferson

The authors of the Constitution trusted Congress would make right and just laws, and the court system would see that every person was treated fairly. However, many people feared the new government would be too strong and, perhaps, take away individual freedom, just as the British government had done.

Therefore, during the fight to ratify the Constitution, the Federalists were obliged to propose a *bill of rights* that would safeguard the people's rights. The Federalists promised this bill of rights would be added to the Constitution as soon as the new Congress met.

As the delegates gathered in May 1787 to revise the Articles of Confederation, a Virginia delegate, George Mason, voiced his disappointment with the new constitutional proposals because "... there is no declaration of individual rights." Mason had earlier written the Virginia Declaration of Rights, and that declaration had influenced Thomas Jefferson when he wrote the first part of the Declaration of Independence. Ultimately, Mason's views were accepted by James Madison. These ideas were coupled with amendments suggested by the states' ratifying conventions.

James Madison

Madison would come to be called the "Father of the Constitution" because of his negotiating power and suggestions of compromise. In 1789, the new Congress took action when Madison proposed 19 amendments. The House of Representatives narrowed those down to 17, with 12 passing the Senate. In 1791, 10 were approved and ratified by the states. They make up what we call the *Bill of Rights*, or the first 10 amendments.

These amendments provide certain guarantees that had not been written into the Constitution. Their purpose was to protect the rights of the people against any misuse of governmental powers. These amendments protect our rights in four general areas. The First Amendment guarantees personal freedom of expression and religion. The next three preserve the security and privacy of every individual. Amendments five through eight are concerned with fair and equal treatment under the law. The last two make general statements guaranteeing that the national government will not take more power than the Constitution grants.

These were the rights the colonists had fought for against the English king, and they did not intend to give them up.

People are guaranteed these freedoms as long as they do not take away the freedom of others. Even today, these important freedoms can be threatened. Controversial subjects are under the protection of the Bill of Rights, such as religion, unpopular ideas, censorship, membership, and activity in unpopular organizations, and expressions of minority opinions. It is the job of the courts to interpret the Constitution and decide the rights of individuals.

It is human nature to believe strongly in one's beliefs and think those holding opposing views must be wrong. Many of us find opinions expressed by others offensive and distressing. We often wish others' opinions could be suppressed. However, we must remember, freedom to express only popular opinions is no freedom at all.

Especially in times of emergency, it is easy to believe that measures infringing upon individual rights can or should be taken "for the good of the country." But this attitude is dangerous to our country since it strikes at the very foundation of our democratic system. More and more rights could be taken away under the justification that it is "for the good of the country."

Before you decide "it doesn't matter" if the rights of someone you do not agree with are violated, stop to consider whether you are willing to risk the loss of your rights because other people disagree with you.

Guaranteed Fundamental Freedoms
The first 10 amendments guarantee:
- freedom of religion, speech, and the press
- the right to assemble and petition the government
- the right to keep and bear arms
- freedom from unreasonable search and seizure
- that no person be deprived of life, liberty, or property without due process of law
- the right to a fair and speedy trial
- the right to a trial by jury
- protection against excessive bail or unusual punishment

QUESTIONS

TRUE OR FALSE? Write a *T* or *F* in the space provided.

____ 1. The first 10 amendments were adopted a month after the Constitution was approved.

____ 2. The first 10 amendments make up the Bill of Rights.

____ 3. Jefferson supported the idea of a bill of rights.

____ 4. The Bill of Rights applies to all levels of government.

____ 5. The Bill of Rights was proposed in an attempt to defeat the Constitution.

____ 6. The Bill of Rights does not give a person the right to criticize a government official.

____ 7. The Bill of Rights protects freedom of speech, even if the speech is unpopular.

____ 8. The right to a trial by jury is in the Bill of Rights.

____ 9. George Mason wrote the Virginia Declaration of Rights.

____ 10. There are times when the courts must interpret the Constitution affecting someone's rights.

____ 11. Congress could choose one religion for the whole country.

____ 12. When the British won the American Revolution they implemented their own Bill of Rights.

Listed below is a sampling of the events that led to America's independence and the adoption of a new constitution. You will find the years and the significant events that happened during that time.

1763 - 1765 Protests Against British Rule

England decides on a program of taxation and control of the colonies. The American colonists begin organized protests against British rule. Patriotic groups such as the *Sons of Liberty* are formed. Laws such as the *Quartering Act*, *Stamp Act*, and *Sugar Act* anger the colonists, who are forced to pay unjust taxes and provide supplies to British troops.

1770 - 1773 Uprisings in Boston

Colonists reduce their boycott of British goods when they withdraw all of the *Townshend Act*, except the tax on tea. *Boston Massacre* (March 5, 1770) occurs when an angry crowd of citizens surrounds a group of soldiers, causing them to open fire. With the American colonists and merchants still angry over British tax policies, an uprising called the *Boston Tea Party* occurs (December 16, 1773).

1774 First Continental Congress

In response to the Boston Tea Party, the Parliament passes several acts to punish Massachusetts. Twelve of the 13 colonies name delegates to *The First Continental Congress*. On September 5th, they convene at *Carpenters Hall* in Philadelphia to deal with Britain's actions.

1775 The American Revolution

When the Americans learn the British plan to seize their guns and ammunition, *Paul Revere* is sent to alert the countryside and gather the *Minutemen*. An unidentified shot triggers the Battle at Lexington. This starts the *American Revolution* and also leads to another famous battle, *Bunker Hill*. In May, the *Second Continental Congress* meets in Philadelphia.

1776 The Declaration of Independence

On July 4th, The Second Continental Congress adopts the *Declaration of Independence* (written by *Thomas Jefferson* and committee). The Declaration was debated by 56 courageous men and signed at *Independence Hall*. A few days later, church bells are rung across Philadelphia to call people to the first public reading of the Declaration.

1777 - 1781 The Articles of Confederation

After considerable debate and alteration, the *Articles of Confederation* were adopted by the Continental Congress on November 15, 1777. However, the document was not fully ratified by the states until March 1, 1781. This document served as the United States' first constitution. In October of 1781, British forces surrender at Yorktown.

1787 - 1788 The Constitution is Ratified

On May 14th, 1787, *The Constitutional Convention* met in Philadelphia. Here the delegates reviewed and approved the *Constitution*. In 1788, nine states ratified the Constitution, and it is put into effect (the remaining four states will ratify by 1790). America prepares to operate under this new document.

1789 Our New Government

On March 4th, the new federal government is inaugurated in New York. In April, the first House of Representatives is organized. *George Washington* is elected the first president on April 6th. He is inaugurated on April 30th. On September 25th, the first 10 amendments (*Bill of Rights*) are adopted by Congress.

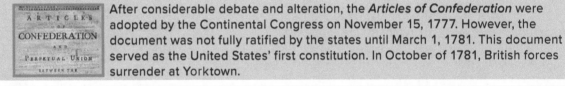

QUESTIONS

PUT THE EVENTS IN ORDER. For each question group, write the numbers *1*, *2*, or *3*, to indicate which event happened first, second, and third.

Group 1. Boston Massacre _____, Adopted Declaration of Independence _____, Washington becomes president _____

Group 2. Articles of Confederation _____, Boston Tea Party _____, Constitution ratified by nine states _____

Group 3. England sets taxation policy for colonies _____, Constitutional Convention _____, Battle of Bunker Hill _____

Group 4. Paul Revere alerts colonists _____, Stamp Act is law _____, First House of Representatives organized _____

Group 5. Bill of Rights adopted _____, First Continental Congress _____, Declaration is read to the public _____

Group 6. Second Continental Congress meets _____, Sons of Liberty forms _____, American Revolution ends _____

The authors of the Constitution could not have imagined that, in 200 years, people would be exploring outer space or going from coast to coast in a few hours. Nor could they have imagined all the changes in daily living that would occur. Today, we claim the protection of the Constitution, written when there were only a few million people in the United States. The Constitution now protects more than 328 million Americans. Almost everything about the United States has changed, except the Constitution. It is truly an outstanding document that has withstood the test of time.

Yet, the Constitution changes in some significant ways. In upcoming units, you will see how the Constitution is officially amended. Officials, who operate the government under the rules of the Constitution, constantly interpret its meaning. The Constitution allows a great deal of freedom to do this (and is referred to as a *living* document). It's a basic guide for the government and safeguards our liberty. It's flexible and brief enough to allow for adjustments. For example, the Constitution sets strict rules for making laws to ensure they are just and democratic. But, the Constitution also gives Congress the power to make laws. This provides our Congress with the ability to make laws in areas that did not even exist when the Constitution was written. Space exploration and the internet are two examples. Can you think of others?

Quotes on the Constitution

Two centuries of growth and unrivaled prosperity have proven the foresight of the 55 men who worked through the summer of 1787 to lay the foundation of the American government. In the words of Archibald Cox, former solicitor general of the United States, "The original Constitution still serves us well despite the tremendous changes in every aspect of American life because the framers had the genius to say enough but not too much.... As the plan outlined in the Constitutional Convention succeeded, as the country grew and prospered both materially and in the realization of its ideals, the Constitution gained majesty and authority far greater than that of any individual or body of men."

Quotes from the Founding Father's give insight into the attitude and mindset of the time:

"Let our government be like that of the solar system. Let the general government be like the sun and the states the planets, repelled yet attracted, and the whole moving regularly and harmoniously in several orbits." — John Dickinson

"The happy Union of these States is a wonder; their Constitution a miracle; their example of Liberty throughout the world." — James Madison

"Our new Constitution is now established, and has an appearance that promises permanency; but in this world nothing can be said to be certain, except death and taxes." — Ben Franklin

"The Constitution is the guide which I will never abandon." — George Washington

Within the Constitution's framework, as interpreted by the courts, we are governed by laws, treaties, and customs. Later, you will study judicial review and the amending process, helping you better understand how the Constitution is changed.

The Constitution has lasted because it:

- provides for a government by the people;
- provides for a government that can act when in danger;
- provides for a federal union where people retain certain rights and powers in their states;
- guarantees individual rights even when the individual's views are unpopular or in the minority;
- has preserved the Union;
- provides the leaders of our government an opportunity to interpret the Constitution and apply it to changing times;
- has provisions for orderly changes.

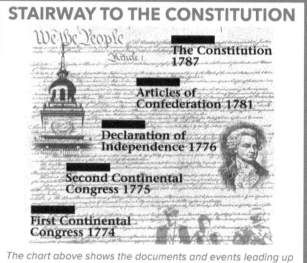

STAIRWAY TO THE CONSTITUTION

We the People

The Constitution 1787

Articles of Confederation 1781

Declaration of Independence 1776

Second Continental Congress 1775

First Continental Congress 1774

The chart above shows the documents and events leading up to the signing of the Constitution in 1787.

QUESTIONS

TRUE OR FALSE? Write a ***T*** or ***F*** in the space provided.

____ 1. Changing the interpretation of the Constitution is what makes our Constitution weak.

____ 2. The Constitution allows laws to be made for subjects that did not exist in 1787.

____ 3. The Constitution can be changed only through rebellion and revolution.

____ 4. Over 500 delegates attended the Constitutional Convention and signed the Constitution.

EVENTS IN ORDER. Write the numbers ***1-4***, indicating which historical event happened first (**1**), second (**2**), third (**3**), or fourth (**4**).

_____ The ratification of the Articles of Confederation.

_____ The adoption of the United States Constitution.

_____ The beginning of the American Revolution.

_____ The signing of the Declaration of Independence.

The Preamble

The Preamble to the United States Constitution comes at the beginning of the document and explains the goals of the Constitution.

"We the people of the United States, in order to form a more perfect Union, establish Justice, insure domestic Tranquility, provide for the common defense, promote the general Welfare, and secure the Blessings of Liberty to ourselves and our Posterity, do ordain and establish this Constitution for the United States of America."

The six reasons for the new government are clearly stated, and the phrase "a more perfect Union" refers to the hope that the Constitution would do a better job than the Articles had done.

A Look Ahead

In this book, you will see the terms *federal*, *national*, and *central*. They all refer to our United States government in Washington, D.C. Our Constitution is a federal constitution. States also have constitutions, but for now, we are studying only the federal Constitution.

In the following pages, you will see that the government has three branches: *executive, legislative,* and *judicial*. You will learn what the president does, how laws are made, how the courts protect us, and many other things about our government. You will also learn how the three branches check each other's powers.

The Constitution can be understood by students who carefully study it. You will probably find you can read and understand many parts of the Constitution yourself. Surely you will find, if you listen to your teacher's directions and instructions, that you are easily able to understand the portions of the Constitution explained in this book. Interesting facts about the Constitution include that it is written on four sheets of paper approximately 28 3/4 inches by 23 5/8 inches.It has 4,543 words, including signatures, and it is the oldest and shortest written constitution of any major government in the world.

As you study, refer to a copy of the Constitution to see each section's exact wording. You will learn about your state government at the end of this study.

Preserving the Constitution

On December 13, 1952, the Constitution and the Declaration of Independence were sealed in helium-filled cases, placed in wooden crates, and transported by an armored car to the National Archives Exhibition Hall in Washington, D.C. Escorting the documents down Pennsylvania and Constitution avenues were two tanks and four servicemen carrying machine guns. Two days later, at a formal ceremony, President Harry Truman declared:

"We are engaged here today in a symbolic act. We are enshrining these documents for future ages. This magnificent hall has been constructed to exhibit them, and the vault beneath, that we have built to protect them, is as safe from destruction as anything that the wit of modern man can devise. All this is an honorable effort, based upon reverence for the great past, and our generation can take just pride in it."

Charters of Freedom

The Rotunda for the *Charters of Freedom* is the permanent home of the Declaration of Independence, Constitution of the United States, and Bill of Rights. These three documents, known collectively as the Charters of Freedom, have secured the rights of the American people for more than two centuries. The rotunda is located in the *National Archives Building* in Washington, D.C., and can be visited by the general public seven days a week (except for Thanksgiving and Christmas).

QUESTIONS

1. What are the six goals in the Preamble?

_____

_____

_____

_____

_____

_____

2. What are some of the words used that refer to the United States government?

_____

_____

3. What are the three branches of government?

_____

_____

4. What is the meaning of the phrase "a more perfect Union"?

_____

_____

_____

DEFINITION PROJECT

You will notice that some of the words in the Preamble are capitalized when normally they would not be. These *key words* are words that the Founders wanted to emphasize. On a separate piece of paper, list and **define these key words** to know if one is to understand the Preamble.

The Constitution consists of the Preamble, seven original articles, and 27 amendments. This summary will aid you in gaining an overview of the Constitution or indexing to find the particular portion of the Constitution that you wish to study. You will find a copy of the entire Constitution on the internet or in the library. Free copies of the federal Constitution and your state constitution are available from the secretary of state in your state capital.

The Seven Articles

The main body of the Constitution is the seven *Articles*. The Articles establish the branches of the federal government and explains how they work. The Articles are the guide to how the federal government interacts with the citizens, states, and people of the country.

  Article 1— Legislative Branch - Outlines the legislative branch, lawmaking requirements for Congress, the elastic clause, and forbidden powers. It is the longest article in the Constitution.

  Article 2 — Executive Branch - Explains the presidential and vice presidential duties, terms of office, succession, impeachment, the oath of office, and specific executive powers.

  Article 3 — Judicial Branch - Addresses the judicial powers of the United States, the Supreme Court and other courts, and specifics about judges. It also defines treason.

  Article 4 — States and the Union - Discuss how the states fit in with the federal government's plan. It sets requirements for new states and conditions of the federal government with respect to states.

  Article 5 — Amendments - This article outlines how to amend the Constitution.

  Article 6 — United States Constitution Supreme - Makes it clear that the federal Constitution is the supreme law of the land.

  Article 7 — Ratifying Procedure - Explains how the Constitution was ratified.

The 27 Amendments

The first 10 amendments were adopted in 1791 and are known as the *Bill of Rights*. A summary of each additional amendment is preceded by the year it was adopted.

No.	Year	Amendment Summary / Highlights
1st	Bill of Rights - 1791 - First 10 Amendments	Freedom of expression, religion, speech, press, assembly, and petition.
2nd		Protects the rights of individual citizens to keep and bear arms. Establishes a militia that is necessary for a free state.
3rd		Prohibits soldiers from temporarily residing (*quartering*) in private homes during peacetime without getting the permission and consent of the owner.

No.	Year	Amendment Summary / Highlights
4th	Bill of Rights - 1791- First 10 Amendments	Protects people's right to privacy, prohibits unreasonable searches and seizures by the government.
5th		No person tried without the grand jury indictment or punished twice for the same offense. Prohibits being a witness against yourself and guarantees "due process of law."
6th		Rights of accused in criminal cases, including legal representation and a fair and speedy trial.
7th		Guarantees a trial by jury.
8th		Insures that punishments for crimes are not excessive, cruel, or unusual.
9th		People retain rights not listed in the United States Constitution.
10th		Power not given to the federal government is given to the people or states (very important for state government).
11th	1795	Individual cannot sue a state in federal courts.
12th	1804	Repeals part of Article 2, Section 1, of the Constitution. Electoral College must cast separate ballots for president and vice president. In 1800, there was difficulty when Thomas Jefferson and Aaron Burr received the same amount of votes in the Electoral College, even though the electors meant Burr's votes to be for the position of vice president. The election had to go to the House of Representatives, where Jefferson won, thanks to the support of Alexander Hamilton. This helps explain why Hamilton and Burr later dueled, and Hamilton was killed.
13th	1865	Abolished slavery and involuntary servitude.
14th	1868	All persons born or naturalized in the United States enjoy full rights. This was done to protect the rights of freed slaves and minorities after the Civil War, but it applies equally to all Americans. This amendment also made specific rules concerning the southern states after the Civil War.
15th	1870	Protects the rights of Americans to vote in elections. States cannot prevent a person from voting because of race, creed, or color. The right to vote is known as *suffrage*.

continued

No.	Year	Amendment Summary / Highlights
16th	1913	Establishes Congress's right to impose a federal income tax.
17th	1913	Provides for popular election of United States senators. Repeals part of Article 1, Section 3. In the past, senators were elected by state legislatures.
18th	1919	*Prohibition*. No alcoholic beverages to be bought or sold in the United States (to be later repealed).
19th	1920	*Woman suffrage*. Some states had already given women the right to vote in some elections. This amendment provides all women, who are U.S. citizens, the right to vote in all elections.
20th	1933	Changed the date the president takes office from March 4th to January 20th (four-year term). It also changed the start of Congress to January 3rd and ended the old second session (end of *Lame Duck Congress*).
21st	1933	Repealed prohibition and voided the 18th Amendment (the only amendment to repeal another amendment).
22nd	1951	No person shall be elected to the office of president more than twice (two terms).
23rd	1961	Gave residents of Washington, D.C., the right to vote in presidential elections.
24th	1964	*Anti-poll tax amendment*. Forbids taxing voters before they vote in national elections.
25th	1967	Established the process by which an ailing president may pass the duties of the office to the vice president and fill the vice president's office, when vacant. Any vacancy in the vice presidency is filled by appointment made by the president, with approval by a majority of both houses of Congress.
26th	1971	18-year-olds are allowed to vote in federal and state elections.
27th	1992	Prohibits Congress from voting itself mid-term pay raises.

Hidden Meanings in the Constitution

The Constitution is filled with hidden techniques and ideas. An example is the election chart (shown in the column to the right) prescribed by the Constitution. It uses different ways to choose some officers, different lengths of a term, and different age requirements. While the president is elected like the members of the Senate and the House, the Electoral College, not the people, actually elect the president. And while the Senate and House are both elected by the people, senators are elected by the vote of all people in the state. Representatives are elected by people from one area of the state. Federal judges are not to be elected by the people at all. These are just some examples.

How do we elect government officials?

	CONGRESS HOUSE	CONGRESS SENATE	PRESIDENT	SUPREME COURT
How Chosen	Elected	Elected	Elected	Appt. by President
Term of Office	2 Years	6 Years	4 Years	Life or Retirement
Age Req.	Minimum 25	Minimum 30	Minimum 35	None

As described in later units, this chart shows that the Constitution affects how elected officials are selected, the terms they serve, and the minimum age requirements.

QUESTIONS

SHORT ANSWER

1. Which article of the Constitution explains the amendment process? _____

2. Where would find the goals of the Constitution? _____ _____

3. The Constitution has a Preamble, _____ original articles, and _____ amendments.

4. The first amendment was passed in _____ , and the last was passed in _____ .

5. Which group of government officials are NOT elected, but rather appointed? _____

MATCH THE AMENDMENT. Write the letter of the corresponding amendment from *Section B* in the space that matches the subject matter in *Section A*.

A

____ 1. 18-year-olds are allowed to vote.

____ 2. Abolished slavery.

____ 3. States cannot prevent a person from voting based on race.

____ 4. All persons born or naturalized in the United States enjoy full rights.

____ 5. Gave all women the right to vote.

____ 6. Limits the number of presidential terms.

____ 7. Guarantees a trial by jury.

____ 8. Prohibits unreasonable searches and seizures.

B

a. 4th	b. 7th	c. 13th	d. 14th
e. 15th	f. 19th	g. 22nd	h. 26th

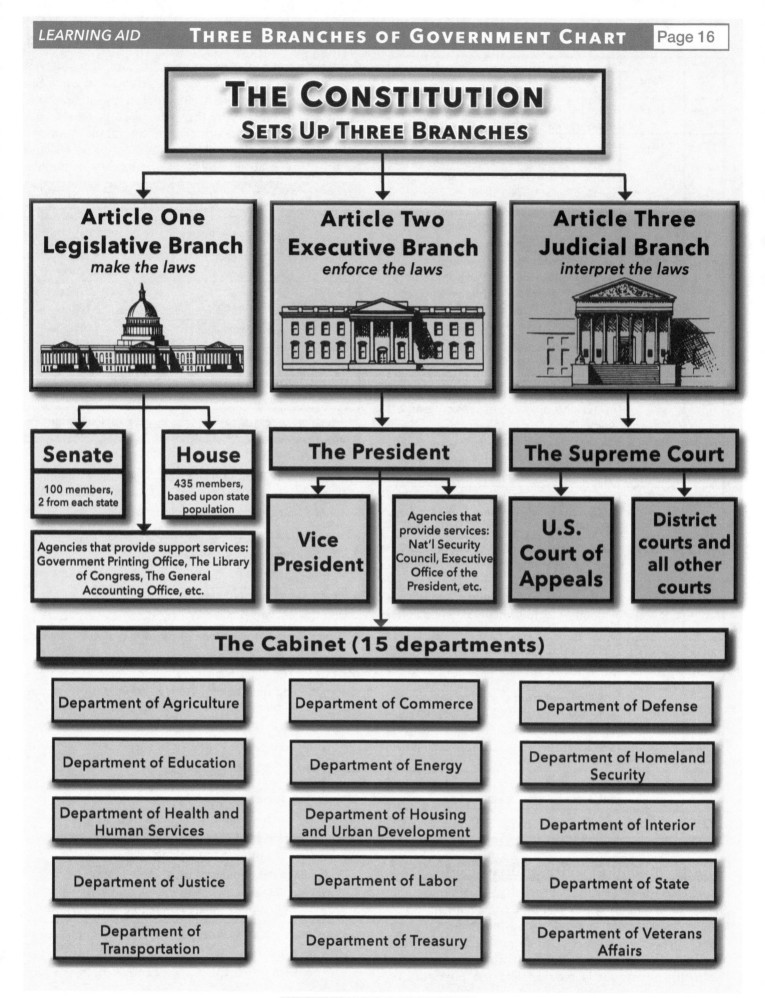

THE CONSTITUTION
SETS UP THREE BRANCHES

Article One
Legislative Branch
make the laws

Article Two
Executive Branch
enforce the laws

Article Three
Judicial Branch
interpret the laws

Senate

100 members, 2 from each state

House

435 members, based upon state population

The President

The Supreme Court

Agencies that provide support services: Government Printing Office, The Library of Congress, The General Accounting Office, etc.

Vice President

Agencies that provide services: Nat'l Security Council, Executive Office of the President, etc.

U.S. Court of Appeals

District courts and all other courts

The Cabinet (15 departments)

Department of Agriculture	Department of Commerce	Department of Defense
Department of Education	Department of Energy	Department of Homeland Security
Department of Health and Human Services	Department of Housing and Urban Development	Department of Interior
Department of Justice	Department of Labor	Department of State
Department of Transportation	Department of Treasury	Department of Veterans Affairs

The legislative branch of government is described in Article 1 of the Constitution. The legislative branch is the first branch mentioned in the Constitution. Its primary duty is to make our country's laws.

The Congress

The legislative branch of our federal government is called the *Congress*. It consists of the Senate and the House of Representatives. Every citizen is represented in Congress by two U.S. senators from their particular state, and one U.S. representative from their congressional district. That is why our form of government is referred to as a *representative government*. The citizens of our great country delegate authority to elected representatives. Although we have more direct representation by our senators and representatives, the same principle is adopted by many executive and judicial offices.

Agencies that provide support services for Congress are also considered part of the legislative branch. They include the Library of Congress, the Congressional Budget Office, the Government Printing Office, and the General Accounting Office.

The term of Congress begins on the third day of January every odd-numbered year, and lasts for two years. The Constitution says that during this two-year term, "Congress shall assemble (meet) at least once in every year..." There is so much business before the Congress these days that the meetings or sessions last almost all year. *Special sessions* of Congress may be called by the President of the United States.

Congress meets in the *Capitol Building* in Washington, D.C. Both the Senate and the House meet there but in different chambers. Pictures of the Capitol Building (see below) are often seen in our newspapers, magazines, and television broadcasts, because the work done in this building is vital to every American. The Capitol is the only place senators and representatives meet to make laws. Senators and representatives have offices nearby. If you visit Washington, D.C., you may attend a session of Congress.

Beginning with the Continental Congress in 1774, America's legislative bodies have kept records of their proceedings. After each day that Congress is in session, the procedures are printed in the *Congressional Record*. This official daily record of the debates and actions of Congress are usually available the following morning on *congress.gov*. The records may include legislative activity by the chambers and their committees, member remarks and speeches, and communications from the president.

Role of Congress

Everyday life is influenced by the decisions of Congress, whose role is to improve the quality of our lives and strengthen the nation. The following are a few of the acts of Congress:

- *air safety* – created the Federal Aviation Agency (FAA), which assures commercial air safety;
- *banking* – established insurance policies, which guarantee deposits made in banks;
- *clean air* – passed national pollution-control laws;
- *family leave* – granted unpaid leave to workers for up to 12 weeks to deal with family issues;
- *labor wages* – created the concept of a federal minimum wage and votes periodic raises;
- *automobile safety* – passed laws to promote auto safety by requiring car manufacturers to meet minimum safety standards;
- *access for the disabled* – expanded employment opportunities for people with disabilities by passing laws requiring access to the workplace and public spaces.

QUESTIONS

1. What is the major duty of the legislative branch?

_____

2. What is the major body in the legislative branch?

_____

3. What two houses make up the legislative branch?

_____

4. What is a representative government? _____

_____

TRUE OR FALSE? Write a *T* or *F* in the space provided.

____ 1. The President of the United States has the power to call Congress into special session.

____ 2. Congress meets in many of our major cities.

____ 3. The Library of Congress is part of the legislative branch.

____ 4. Congress must meet at least twice every year.

____ 5. The president makes the rules for Congress.

____ 6. Congress meets in the Capitol Building in Washington, D.C.

____ 7. The daily record of Congress is called "The Capital Journal."

The Capitol Building - The Meeting Place of Congress

The Senate

The Senate of the United States is discussed in Article 1, Section 3, of the Constitution.

The Senate has 100 members: two from each of the 50 states. As you recall, there was a dispute between the small states and the large states at the Constitutional Convention. The Senate was designed to calm that debate by making all states equal. Every state, regardless of size, has two members. Indiana's two Republican senators are Todd Young (term expires 2023) and Mike Braun (term expires 2025).

Todd Young   *Mike Braun*

Of the 100 senators, one-third are elected every two years for six-year terms. Terms are staggered this way, so only one-third of the Senate goes out of office at any one time. This assures the Senate will have experienced members at all times. Each one-third of the Senate is called a class. All senators serve six-year terms.

class	have served	years to serve	comments
1	0	6	just elected
2	2	4	elected 2 years ago
3	4	2	elected 4 years ago
	6	0	were just up for re-election and were re-elected or replaced by class 1

U.S. Senate Chart of Election

Senators may be re-elected for an unlimited number of terms. This is not uncommon; many have had long careers.

Senate Salary, Qualifications, & Vacancy

A senator receives a salary of $174,000 and an expense allowance. A senator must be at least 30 years old, a United States citizen for at least nine years, and a resident of the state he/she represents in the Senate.

If a Senate vacancy occurs, the governor of the state affected makes a temporary appointment until the next election. This appointment is a very important duty for the governor.

Officers of the Senate

The Vice President of the United States is the *president of the Senate*. This is established by the Constitution. Since the vice president is the second highest official in the executive branch of government and the Senate is part of the legislative branch, this is one way in which the two branches are drawn closer.

Although the vice president is the presiding officer of the Senate, this official may not debate or vote except in the case of a tie. The Senate also elects one of its members to be *president pro tempore*. The president pro tempore serves in the absence of the vice president. There are also Senate *majority* and *minority leaders*. The Senate majority and minority leaders and the president pro tempore receive a salary of $193,400.

Senate Duties

The Senate passes *bills* (a term for proposed laws) it hopes will become laws according to a plan you will read about shortly. According to this plan, the House of Representatives must also pass the bill before it is sent to the president for approval.

This group also has the vital role of approving treaties made by the president. It also approves the selection of certain federal officers by the president.

The Senate is the jury in cases of *impeachment*. Impeachment is the political process of leveling charges against public officials of wrongdoing from office. The impeachment process was included in Article 2, Section 4 of the U.S. Constitution: "The President, Vice President and all civil Officers of the United States, shall be removed from Office on Impeachment for, and Conviction of, Treason, Bribery, or other high Crimes and Misdemeanors." The purpose is to protect the public from officials who are unfit to wield power. If a president is tried for impeachment, the chief justice of the Supreme Court presides over the trial.

Impeachment of U.S. Presidents

Our founding fathers wanted impeachment to be a lengthy and complicated process. So it is hard to remove any official from office, and that is by design. Impeachment has only been used four times against a sitting president. While many U.S. presidents have been threatened with impeachment, Congress has only conducted three presidential impeachment trials, *Andrew Johnson (1868)*, *Bill Clinton (1998)*, and *Donald Trump (2019)*. They were all acquitted after trials in the Senate. *Richard Nixon (1974)* resigned before facing a House impeachment vote.

Electing Senators

The 17th Amendment changed the way we elect senators. If you look at Article 1, Section 3, of the Constitution, you will see state legislatures originally had the power to elect senators. A look at the 17th Amendment will show that the people of the states now have that power. Senators are not elected by district since they represent the entire state.

continued

House of Representatives

The House of Representatives is discussed in Article 1, Section 2 of the Constitution. The House of Representatives has 435 members from various states. This number is fixed by law. Each state is given its share of the 435 members according to population. Going back to the Constitutional Convention, this house of Congress favored the large states in their dispute with the small states since large states receive more members.

Each state has at least one representative, and the largest state has more than 50 members. Based on Census 2020 results for the 118th Congress, some states have gained congressional seats, and some have lost seats. Indiana has nine U.S. House seats, and that number was unchanged after the census. The reapportioned 118th Congress will convene in January 2023 (based upon the 2022 midterm elections). Voters elect representatives from their state district.

All members of the House of Representatives are elected every two years for two-year terms. Members are elected at the general election held in their states in November of even-numbered years. They take office on January 3rd of the odd-numbered years. Representatives may be elected an unlimited number of times.

House Salary, Qualifications, & Vacancy

A representative receives a salary of $174,000 and an expense allowance. A representative must be at least 25 years of age, a U.S. citizen for at least seven years, and an inhabitant of the state he/she represents.

A vacancy in the office of a representative is filled by a *special election* called by the governor of the state affected.

House Officers

Speaker Nancy Pelosi

The presiding officer of the House of Representatives is the speaker of the House, elected by the majority party. Nancy Pelosi (D-California) is the only woman to have served as speaker, and was elected speaker for a fourth time when the 117th Congress convened on January 3, 2021. The speaker's salary is $223,500, plus an expense allowance. There is also a House minority and House majority leader elected from the minority and majority parties. Both receive a salary of $193,400.

House Duties

The primary duty of the House is to pass bills it hopes will become laws. The Senate must pass the same bills before they are sent to the president for final approval. All bills for revenue must start in the House.

The Constitution provides that the House "shall have the sole Power of Impeachment," meaning the power to bring impeachment charges against any federal officer. After the House charges an official, the Senate decides the case.

The House also has the critical duty of selecting a president if no candidate has a majority in the Electoral College.

Rules and Privileges

Congress may expel or punish its members. It makes the rules about its procedures and keeps records of all meetings. Members are privileged from arrest while going to or coming from Congress or while attending a session. However, if they commit a criminal offense, they may be arrested. A member of Congress may not be sued for what he or she says in Congress, but Congress may make specific rules about proper behavior and speech of its members.

The House and Congress Number

Congress gets a new number each time the House of Representatives starts a new term. Therefore, every two years, we have a new Congress. For example, the House that began its term in 2021 was the 117th Congress, and in 2023, the 118th Congress will meet.

Women in Government

As a result of the 2020 general elections, a record number of women will serve in the 117th Congress. There will be 24 women serving in the Senate and 116 serving in the House, including six new women of color in Congress. Democrats Cori Bush will be Missouri's first Black congresswoman, and Nikema Williams was elected to the late Representative John Lewis' seat in Georgia.

Census

Article 1 of the Constitution requires that our country's *census* (count) be taken every 10 years. The census most recently took place in 2020, with the next census taking place in 2030. This count is managed by a government agency called the U.S. Bureau of the Census. The census serves many purposes. The three most important being:

1. The census tells us about the makeup of our large American population and how the government and businesses might serve the population. Your state and local governments will use this information to plan for schools, hospitals, roads, and more.

2. It tells the federal government how federal money should be divided between states and local areas.

3. The government uses this information to outline voting districts in each state and decide how many state and U.S. representatives each state receives. An adjustment to legislative districts based upon population change is called reapportionment. Reapportionment leads to redistricting, the redrawing of congressional district boundaries.

The 2020 final census numbers show America continuing the population shift from the Northeast and Midwest to the South and West, a trend that will shape Congress for the next decade. The political power in the industrial belt stretching from New York to Illinois is once again losing seats in Congress while Sun Belt states such as Florida, North Carolina, and Texas will gain them. California will lose a seat for the first time.

QUESTIONS

SENATE/HOUSE COMPARISON. Fill in the blank with *Senate (S)*, *House (H)*, *both (B)* or *neither (N)*.

____ 1. Approves or rejects treaties.

____ 2. Starts all revenue bills.

____ 3. Passes bills they hope will become laws.

____ 4. This group has 100 members.

____ 5. Designed to favor small states.

____ 6. This group has 435 members.

____ 7. Are elected by the people of the entire state.

____ 8. The speaker is the chief officer.

____ 9. Approve nominations made by the president.

____ 10. The vice president is the chief officer.

____ 11. Bring impeachment charges against an official.

____ 12. Serves as the jury in cases of impeachment.

____ 13. Members are elected every two years.

____ 14. Meet in the Capitol Building.

____ 15. Vacancies are filled by appointment from the state governor.

____ 16. Discussed in Article 1, Section 3 of Constitution.

____ 17. The census affects the number of members per state.

____ 18. Congress consists of this group(s).

SHORT ANSWER (SENATE) - Answer the questions involving the U.S. Senate.

1. How many senators are there? _____

2. How many from each state? _____

3. How long is a Senate term? _____

4. How many, fraction and approximate number, are elected every two years? _____

5. What are the qualifications for a senator? _____

6. Name three duties of the Senate. _____

7. Who is the presiding officer of the Senate? _____

8. Each third of the Senate is called a _____ .

9. What is the salary of a senator? _____

10. Name one of the two senators from your state.

SHORT ANSWER (HOUSE) - Answer the questions involving the U.S. House of Representatives.

1. What are the qualifications for a representative?

2. In which article and section of the Constitution will you find information about the House?

3. Who is the speaker of the House of Representatives?

4. How many representatives in Congress? _____

5. How many representatives from your state? _____

6. What is the present number of Congress?

7. What happens if there is a vacancy in the House?

8. What is the salary of a representative? _____

TRUE OR FALSE? Write a *T* or *F* in the space provided.

____ 1. The number of women in Congress is decreasing.

____ 2. The governor fills a temporary vacancy in the office of a senator.

____ 3. The makeup of the Senate favors the large states.

____ 4. The 22nd Amendment changed the way we select a senator.

____ 5. A senator may be re-elected an unlimited number of times.

____ 6. There are times when members of Congress may not be arrested.

____ 7. There is an even split between men and women in the U.S. House, each accounting for 50 percent.

____ 8. Representatives serve two-year terms.

____ 9. Each state must have at least four representatives.

____ 10. Representatives take office the day after an election.

____ 11. The House is not involved with impeachment.

____ 12. Under unique circumstances, the House appoints the President of the United States.

____ 13. The vice president is a valuable link between the executive branch and the legislative branch.

____ 14. Representatives may be re-elected for an unlimited number of terms.

____ 15. Senators are elected from the state as a whole; representatives are elected from districts in the state.

____ 16. The number of Congress changes every six years.

____ 17. All revenue bills must start in the House.

____ 18. The population of a state affects the number of representatives it receives.

____ 19. The next census will take place in 2025.

EXPRESS YOUR OPINION

A senator said, "A legislator should listen to everyone affected by a bill before voting on it." Should a legislator always vote the way he or she feels is best? Or should legislators vote according to what the majority of the people want? What do you think?

"Every bill which shall have passed the House of Representatives and the Senate, shall, before it becomes law, be presented to the President of the United States...." —— United States Constitution, Article 1

Powers to make laws are given to Congress, consisting of the Senate and House of Representatives. Our nation needs rules and regulations to protect our safety and ensure our rights as citizens. A description of the lawmaking powers can be found in Article 1 of the Constitution.

In both houses of Congress, no business may be transacted without a *quorum*. A quorum in each house is a majority of its members. A majority is one-half plus one.

How a Bill Becomes Law in Congress

Bills, a term for proposed laws, may start in either house of Congress Bills for *revenue* must begin in the House of Representatives (see Article 1, Section 7). After a bill is introduced, it is given a number and usually referred to a *special committee*. There are 16 Senate committees and 24 House committees, plus four special or select Senate committees.

In a committee, detailed studies are made of the bill, and hearings may be held. A committee may amend, rewrite, recommend passage, or ignore a bill. It is possible to pass some bills without committee approval, but this seldom happens. Some people feel these committees are too powerful and may keep members of Congress from considering certain laws. Committees are necessary, however, and Congress determines rules controlling their behavior and power.

Thousands of bills are introduced during a session of Congress. Four out of five of these bills have little or no chance of being passed into law. Bills that seem unimportant to the committees are ignored. The bills that are taken seriously may have public hearings. After the committee finishes with a bill, it is reported to the Senate or House favorably or unfavorably. The entire Senate or House then votes on the bill.

The bills that come from committees are put on a calendar and voted on according to a schedule. Changes to the bill may be made, and then the final vote is taken. The bill is sent to the other house of Congress if the vote is favorable.

In the other house of Congress, the same type of procedure is followed. If the other house passes the bill, but with changes, a joint committee from both houses is set up to work out a *compromise bill*.

After the bill has passed both houses, it is sent to the president, who may either sign or veto it. This particular duty is found in Article 1, Section 7, of the Constitution. If the president signs the bill, it becomes another law of our land. If the president does not sign the bill but vetoes it, the two houses of Congress may try to override the president's veto by a two-thirds vote in each house. Very few laws are passed this way.

If the president does not act at all, the bill becomes law automatically in 10 days, providing Congress is still in session. If Congress adjourns before the 10-day period is up and the president has not acted on the bill, it is automatically vetoed. This is called a *pocket veto*.

continued

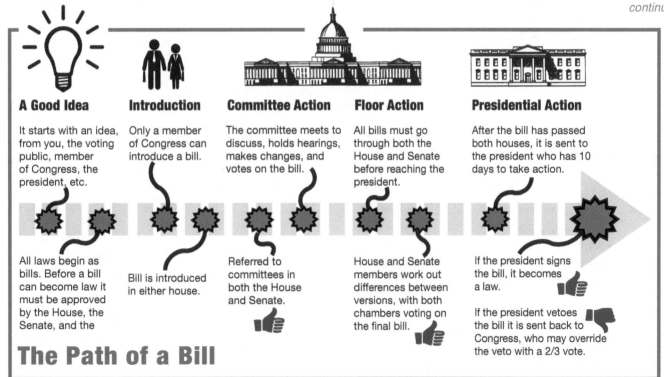

The Path of a Bill

A Good Idea
It starts with an idea, from you, the voting public, member of Congress, the president, etc.

All laws begin as bills. Before a bill can become law it must be approved by the House, the Senate, and the

Introduction
Only a member of Congress can introduce a bill.

Bill is introduced in either house.

Committee Action
The committee meets to discuss, holds hearings, makes changes, and votes on the bill.

Referred to committees in both the House and Senate.

Floor Action
All bills must go through both the House and Senate before reaching the president.

House and Senate members work out differences between versions, with both chambers voting on the final bill.

Presidential Action
After the bill has passed both houses, it is sent to the president who has 10 days to take action.

If the president signs the bill, it becomes a law.

If the president vetoes the bill it is sent back to Congress, who may override the veto with a 2/3 vote.

Lawmaking and the Three Branches

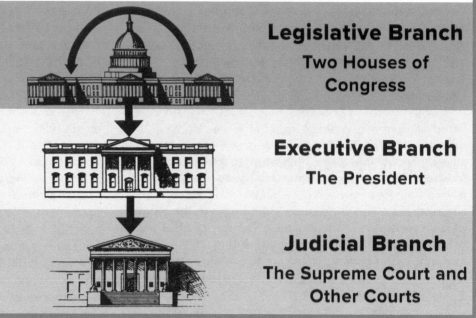

A bill is introduced, sent to committee, then voted on. If passed in committee and later on the floor of the house, it is sent to the other house.

Legislative Branch
Two Houses of Congress

The president may sign the bill, and it will become law or may decide to veto. Congress may try to pass it over the veto by a two-thirds vote.

Executive Branch
The President

The courts see that justice is administered under the law. The Supreme Court may declare laws unconstitutional.

Judicial Branch
The Supreme Court and Other Courts

After Congress (legislative branch) has passed a bill and the president (executive branch) has signed it into law, it is the president's duty to enforce the law. The courts (judicial branch) then interpret it and administer justice under it. The Supreme Court may rule whether or not the law is constitutional.

What are Federal Laws?

There are different types of laws. Federal laws apply to everyone in the United States. States and local laws apply to people who live or work in a particular state, county, or municipality. The U.S. Constitution divides the power to make laws between the federal and state government.

The federal government is responsible for some types of laws, such as those pertaining to national defense, currency, interstate commerce, patents, and so forth. State and local governments may not pass these kinds of laws, nor may they pass laws that conflict with federal laws. One example is the 14th Amendment to the U.S. Constitution, which ensures the Bill of Rights applies to all states. You will learn more about the differences between federal, state, and local laws in the upcoming units of this book.

Member of Congress: Typical Day

Regardless of whether they are in Washington, D.C., or their congressional districts, members of Congress spend most of their time working. Members work long hours, up to 70 hours a week when Congress is in session. Members endure unequaled public scrutiny and sacrifice family time to fulfill work responsibilities.

A member of Congress may have a typical day something like this:

7:00 a.m. Breakfast with the family, the only time they will see each other until late that evening.

8:00 a.m. Trip to the office to go over e-mail and postal mail with an assistant. The mail may be substantial if a critical issue is pending.

10:15 a.m. Meet with party members considering action on a bill that will come before Congress.

10:30 a.m. House Ethics Committee meeting. This committee, which is his/her most important committee assignment, may discuss new allegations of concern to Congress. Both senators and representatives may have more than one committee assignment.

11:00 a.m. A party caucus (meeting) takes place.

Noon Lunch with other members from his/her home state. Congressional business is discussed.

1:30 p.m. On the way to the House floor, he/she is stopped by the majority leader for a brief discussion of important bills.

1:40 p.m. Remains on the floor for the entire afternoon House of Representatives session, voting on legislation.

3:30 p.m. Conduct a short conference call with other lawmakers concerning a defense bill.

3:45 p.m. Lobbyist John Jones comes to the office seeking aid favorable to their organization.

5:00 p.m. A reporter calls for an interview concerning the House Ethics Committee.

7:00 p.m. Home for dinner. After dinner reads hometown newspapers, reads topics on social media, and works on a speech to be delivered the next day.

The Politics of Lawmaking

Although the charts on the previous pages show the lawmaking process, it does not reflect how complicated this process is. Many informal conversations and discussions take place with members of Congress. Each wants to voice his or her position, learn what arguments opponents will use, and make the necessary adjustments to help get a bill passed. Members of Congress must understand the president's view on the legislation and the political impacts of the bill. A representative who votes for or against a controversial bill will have that on his or her voting record.

There are several terms that you should research that involve strategy and agreements that lawmakers use. These include *filibustering*, *logrolling*, *pork-barrel spending*, and *pigeonholing*, to name a few.

Lobbies in Washington, D.C.

Our lawmakers in Congress feel the effect of *political action committees* (PACs), special-interest groups, and lobbies. PACs and special-interest groups are individuals interested in particular goals. Lobbies are the active parts of these groups that seek to influence our legislators.

Lobbies are controlled by law, and most operate legally. Some even provide helpful service to legislators by informing them how certain groups feel about important issues. However, a legislator must be careful that these lobbies do not exert too much influence over them and that other Americans' views are not overlooked.

It is the right and duty of organized groups to let their legislators know their opinions on legislative matters, but keeping these groups within proper bounds is essential.

Lobbyists are hired by companies involved in areas such as finance and banking, construction, defense, organized labor, health care, transportation, and energy. The specific topics may involve gun politics, proper use of the environment, immigration, energy sources, and regulations surrounding the banking industry.

Liberals, Conservatives, and Extremists

Often when reading about Congress and politics, you will find the terms *liberal*, *conservative*, or *extremist*. A *liberal* is someone who believes the national government should be very active in helping individuals and communities promote health, education, justice, and equal opportunity. Twentieth-century presidents who would be known as liberals include Democrats Franklin D. Roosevelt and John F. Kennedy.

A *conservative* is someone who believes that the role of government in society should be minimal and that individuals should be responsible for their well-being. Twentieth-Century presidents who would be known as conservatives include Republicans Richard Nixon and Ronald Reagan.

Both conservatives and liberals have played a large part in the success of our nation. Both liberal and conservative views have merit, and the honest political debate between them has been good for our country. In many instances, workable compromises between the two views have been found.

An *extremist* is someone who stops at nothing to get his or her political way. They would ruin the reputations of political enemies, lie, cheat, steal, or even kill. The 1995 bombing in Oklahoma City and the 9/11 events are examples of extremist activity. Extremism is a threat to our Constitution, laws, and society. There is no justification for extremism.

The Internet and Lawmaking

The internet is now the primary source for learning about legislation and contacting members of Congress. One way to find your legislators' official social media contacts is through their websites. Social media, of course, does not replace the traditional methods of constituent communications, but some – particularly, Twitter, Facebook, blogs, and YouTube – are now essential for public officials.

These new means of communicating allow for quicker sharing of information, which may include:

- *position taking* - their position on a policy or issue;
- *upcoming schedule* - events of interest to constituents;
- *direct responses to citizens* - allows quick response to citizens' questions or concerns.

Your Participation in Lawmaking

The U.S. government is the basis for participatory democracy, which Abraham Lincoln described as a government made "of the people, by the people, and for the people." Under the Constitution, U.S. citizens have the right to influence public policy and lawmaking.

You may voice your opinions through written letters or emails, which are the most popular method of communicating with your representatives. The following are suggestions for writing a powerful message:

- state the purpose of your letter in the first few sentences;
- be polite and concise, include key information, and use examples to support your position;
- keep the message brief, one page is ideal, and discuss only one issue per letter or email;
- give your full name, along with your mailing and email addresses;
- indicate if you are a member of an organization interested in the proposed legislation.

QUESTIONS

FILL IN THE BLANKS / SHORT ANSWER

1. In Congress, where are bills sent for consideration?

_____

2. What is the president's role in lawmaking?

_____

_____

_____

3. What is a pocket veto? _____

_____

4. Which group of Congress has more members, the Senate or House? _____

5. After a bill has passed the two houses of _____, it is sent to the _____.

TRUE OR FALSE? Write a *T* or *F* in the space provided.

____ 1. The Congress vetoes laws.

____ 2. The Supreme Court helps in making laws.

____ 3. Bills may start in either house of Congress.

____ 4. Revenue bills start in the Senate.

____ 5. A three-fourth vote is necessary for Congress to override a president's veto.

____ 6. The president can declare laws unconstitutional.

____ 7. Lobbies are illegal in Washington, D.C.

____ 8. After a law is passed, if it is in conflict with the Constitution, it can be made void by the Supreme Court.

WHICH BRANCH? Answer *Executive (E)*, *Legislative (L)*, or *Judicial (J)* branch.

____ 1. Makes the country's laws.

____ 2. Enforces the country's laws.

____ 3. Tries cases under the laws.

____ 4. Is the court system of the country.

____ 5. Has two houses.

____ 6. The president is the head of this branch.

____ 7. The Supreme Court is the chief body.

____ 8. Members are not elected.

____ 9. Uses pocket veto.

____ 10. Uses joint committees.

LAWMAKING BY THE NUMBERS. Choose the correct number from the number bank that matches the statement.

Number Bank: 1/2, 2/3, 1, 2, 4, 6, 8, 10, 50, 100, 435

____ Lawmaking in this Article of the Constitution.

____ President has this many days to take action.

____ Number of U.S. senators in Congress.

____ Number of U.S. representatives in Congress.

____ A U.S. representative's term in years.

____ Fraction of votes Congress needs to override a veto.

LEARNING AID	**LEGISLATIVE BRANCH FACT SHEET**
Main Body	Congress, consisting of a *Senate and House of Representatives*
Membership	*Senate:* 100 *House of Representatives:* 435
Terms of Office	*Senate:* 6 years *House of Representatives:* 2 years
Salaries	*Senate:* $174,000 majority and minority Leaders, president pro tempore: $193,400 *House of Representatives:* $174,000 speaker of the House: $223,500
Requirements	*Senate:* 30 years old, a citizen for 9 years, resident of the state represented. *House of Representatives:* 25 years old, a citizen for 7 years, resident of the state represented.
Officers	*Senate:* President of the Senate (Vice President of the United States), president pro tempore, majority leader, minority leader. *House of Representatives:* speaker of the House, majority leader, minority leader.
Meeting Place	Capitol Building, Washington, D.C.
Duties	Main duty of the legislative branch is to make laws. *Senate:* Pass bills, decide guilt of impeached federal officers, approve presidential appointments, approve treaties. *House of Representatives:* Pass bills, charge federal officers in impeachment cases, select president when no candidate has a majority in the Electoral College, start all revenue bills. *Joint Duties:* Raise, borrow, and coin money; have defense powers; control immigration; grant copyrights and patents; control commerce; govern Washington, D.C.; investigate executive branch. *Forbidden Powers:* No ex post facto laws, no suspension of habeas corpus, no tax on exports, no title of nobility, no bill of attainder, no mid-term pay raises.
Article Number	Article 1 of the U.S. Constitution

The material discussed on this page concerns Article 1, Sections 8 and 9, of the Constitution and the various amendments.

Powers of Congress

The Senate and House of Representatives have several duties besides making laws and besides the ones listed previously (impeachment, appointment approval, etc.). Eighteen powers are given to Congress by the Constitution (see *enumerated powers* below). These powers can be roughly classified into three groups:

1. **Money** – Congress' most significant power lies in the fact that it holds the nation's purse strings. Congress has the authority to raise, borrow, and coin money and set the value of money. Raising money is achieved by collecting taxes and borrowing through the sale of government bonds. Coining money is the task of the Treasury Department.
2. **Defense** – Powers relating to defense include powers for raising and supporting the armed forces. Only Congress has the authority to declare war.
3. **Miscellaneous** – Congress regulates immigration and issues copyrights to protect the creations of writers and composers. Congress also governs commerce between states and between the United States and foreign countries. If you remember some of the trade difficulties under the Articles of Confederation, you know why Congress has these commerce powers.

Congress also governs the District of Columbia (Washington, D.C.). It does so to ensure that the United States' capital will be run in the best interest of all Americans.

Elastic Clause

The most all-inclusive power granted by the Constitution to Congress is found in Article 1, Section 8, Clause 18. After spelling out the duties of Congress, the authors realized situations might arise that are not covered under the provisions of the Constitution. Therefore, a clause called the *elastic clause* states that Congress shall "make all laws which shall be necessary for carrying into execution the foregoing powers." It makes the Constitution a living document, giving Congress powers that are "necessary and proper" to run the government.

Briefly, this means that Congress has the authority to make all laws necessary to carry out the Constitution's spirit, as outlined in Article 1. This clause has been used to cover several areas, and situations never dreamed of by the members of the Constitutional Convention. Powers expressed in the Constitution are called *expressed* or *enumerated powers*. Powers that are not expressed but believed to be a power of the Congress are called *implied powers*. The power to declare war and establish post offices are expressed powers (look ahead on Page 26 for others). The power to regulate TV stations, nuclear energy, and the airlines are implied powers.

Things Congress Cannot Do

Besides things Congress can do, the Constitution lists a few things Congress cannot do. The powers denied Congress are specified in a shortlist in Article I, Section 9. Combine these with various amendments, and especially the Bill of Rights, for the specific prohibitions in the Constitution.

For instance, Congress cannot pass a law that turns an act into a crime after the act was committed. This type of law is called an ex post facto law. An example would be a woman who receives a ticket for parking on Main Street on Monday when there is no law against it. When she arrives in court later in the week, she finds a law was passed on Tuesday, and she is being punished for parking on Monday. Obviously, this would not be fair. This type of law was used by unjust kings to trap their enemies.

No person holding a federal office is permitted to accept a title of nobility, such as duke, earl, etc., from a foreign country. No member of Congress may receive a gift from a foreign country without Congress' consent.

Congress cannot suspend the writ of habeas corpus except under special circumstances. Habeas corpus is a Latin term meaning "you shall have the body." It is an order to a jailer to bring a prisoner to a court or to set the prisoner free. Without habeas corpus, prisoners could be detained almost permanently without a trial. Congress is also not permitted to pass a bill of attainder. A bill of attainder is an act passed by a legislature to punish a person or group without a trial.

Congress cannot tax any goods exported from any state, whether the goods are going to another state or a foreign country. This provision for no export taxes comes from weaknesses in the Articles of Confederation. Under the Articles, states had been taxing each other harmfully, and commerce was at a standstill. States are also prohibited from taxing business.

Neither the Senate nor the House of Representatives may adjourn or move to another location without the consent of the other house. These denials of power came about either as a result of the misuses of power under the Articles of Confederation or under British rule.

The 27th Amendment, which was the last amendment passed (in 1992), prohibits Congress from voting itself a pay raise during its term in office.

U.S. Congress vs. State Legislature

It is easy for students to confuse the elected officials in the state legislature with those who work for them in the U.S. Congress (Washington, D.C.). The table below further explains the differences, many of which will be covered in the federal and state sections of this book. Both Congress and your state legislature have a two-body system referred to as a *bicameral system*. The only exception is the Nebraska Legislature, which is *unicameral* (one body).

Topic	U.S. Congress	State Legislature
Lawmaking Scope	Federal level - creating laws for all 50 states	State level - creating laws for only Indiana
Lawmaking Bodies	U.S. Senate & U.S. House of Representatives	Indiana Senate & Indiana House of Representatives
Number of Members	100 U.S. Senators (2 from each state) & 435 U.S. Representatives (9 from Indiana)	50 members of the state Senate and 100 members of the state House of Representatives
Meeting Place	Washington, D.C.	State Capital (Indianapolis) and in their legislative district
Examples of Scope	National defense, federal tax policies, immigration laws	Funding schools, state environmental issues, state taxing
Speed of Legislation	More formal process, taking on larger issues, longer legislative sessions	Generally quicker passage, shorter legislative sessions

The Two Chambers

The two-chamber design of the U.S. Congress is consistent with the basic principle of government used by the framers of our Constitution: that the government must be divided into units which share power. The two chambers are considered equal, although they differ from one another in many respects. The Senate has sometimes been called the *upper body* and the House the *lower body*. These are popular misnomers that started when Congress first met in New York City; the Senate chamber was on the floor above the House. As we know, both legislative bodies are equal.

QUESTIONS

TRUE OR FALSE? Write a *T* or *F* in the space provided.

___ 1. Coining and printing money are the responsibilities of the Treasury Department.

___ 2. An ex post facto law is a law that makes an act illegal after the act has been committed.

___ 3. Only federal officials may have titles of nobility.

___ 4. Congress cannot tax goods being exported from a state, even if the goods are going to a foreign country.

___ 5. Article 1 of the U.S. Constitution outlines the legislative branch and the powers of Congress.

___ 6. Any of the three branches of government may declare war.

___ 7. The Senate and the House are prohibited from adjourning without the consent of the other.

___ 8. Congress does not govern the independent region of the District of Columbia.

___ 9. Although the state legislature meets in the state capitol, it makes laws for all 50 states.

IMPLIED, EXPRESSED, OR DENIED? Identify each of the following as an implied (*IM*), expressed (*EX*), or denied (*DN*) power of Congress in the space provided.

___ 1. Collect taxes.

___ 2. Declare war.

___ 3. Regulate the Internet.

___ 4. Provide for punishment of counterfeiters.

___ 5. Grant patents and copyrights.

___ 6. Regulate satellite communications.

___ 7. Grant titles of nobility.

___ 8. Establish post offices.

___ 9. Pass ex post facto laws.

DEFINE

1. expressed powers _____

_____

2. implied powers _____

_____

3. prohibits _____

_____

4. bill of attainder _____

_____

5. export _____

_____

6. bicameral _____

_____

FILL IN THE BLANKS

1. The Senate is referred to as the_____body, and the House is called the _____ body.

2. Revenue bills must begin in the_____.

3. The _____ has been used by Congress in writing laws about things not directly mentioned in the Constitution.

4. Congress' power can be roughly divided into three groups: _____

_____

SEQUENCE OF A BILL - Put the lawmaking events in sequence from first to last as they relate to a proposed bill.

a. president acts on the bill and approves

b. bill is a law and is communicated to the public

c. bill is submitted to first house for review

d. sponsor introduces bill

e. bill passes both houses of Congress

f. referred to and discussed in committee

How the Federal Government and States Divide Powers

The Constitution Says...

Certain Powers Belong to the Federal Government:

★ Regulate Interstate Commerce

★ Conduct Foreign Affairs

★ Coin and Issue Money

★ Establish Post Offices

★ Make War and Peace

★ Maintain Armed Forces

★ Admit New States and Govern Territories

★ Punish Crimes Against the U.S.

★ Grant Patents and Copyrights

★ Make Uniform Laws on Naturalization and Bankruptcy

(Also considered expressed powers.)

Certain Powers Belong to State Governments:

(Mainly comes from an interpretation of the reserved powers.)

★ Authorize Establishment of Local Governments

★ Establish and Supervise Schools

★ Provide for State Militia

★ Regulate Commerce Within the State

★ Charter Corporations

★ Regulate Labor, Industry, and Business Within the State

★ All Other Powers Not Delegated to the United States Government or Specifically Prohibited to the States

Certain Powers Are Shared by Both Governments

Tax...Establish Courts...Promote Agriculture and Industry...Borrow Money...
Charter Banks...Protect the Public Health...Provide For Public Welfare

Certain Powers Are Prohibited to Both Governments

The personal rights of citizens of the United States, as listed in the Bill Of Rights (first 10 amendments to the Constitution) and in state constitutions, cannot be reduced or destroyed by the federal or the state governments. Also, certain specific prohibitions in the Constitution itself, such as no title of nobility, no ex post facto laws, no duty on exports, no bill of attainder, etc.

"This great principle is, that the Constitution and the laws...are supreme; that they control the Constitution and the laws of the respective states and cannot be controlled by them." —— John Marshall, Supreme Court Justice in 1801

Relationship Among States

The Constitution has something to say about how the states should act toward each other and the federal government. For example, in Article 4, there is the *full faith and credit clause*. Under this clause, every state must accept the statutes, records, and decisions of all other states. The forefathers of our country intended that no person shall be able to dodge their obligations in the United States by just moving to another location within the United States.

In criminal cases, a criminal found in a different state must be returned to the state where the crime was committed by a process called *extradition*. Because each state must accept the statutes of another state, we sometimes find people crossing state lines for court decisions when it works to their advantage, as in some marriages and divorces.

Each state must treat the citizens of other states the same as it treats its citizens. There cannot be special laws for those who are from other states. This directive is given in Article 4, Section 2.

The federal government must guarantee all states a republican form of government and must guarantee to protect them from invasion. Also, a state may call for federal assistance to prevent domestic violence. In this paragraph, a "republican form of government" means a constitutional and democratic form of government.

The Constitution specifies duties that may only be performed by the federal government. For example, Article 1, Section 10, explains that states cannot coin money, make treaties, grant titles of nobility, pass *ex post facto laws* (as discussed on the previous page, a law that retroactively changes the legal consequences of acts committed), or impair obligation of contracts. Article 1, Section 8, lists the powers of Congress and shows that the states cannot use any of these powers.

Powers of the States

Since the Constitution does not list in detail the powers belonging to the states, there have been many conflicts over their respective powers. The 10th Amendment clarifies that any powers not delegated by the Constitution to the federal government are reserved to the states or the people. These are called *reserved powers*.

However, anything not forbidden by the Constitution or given to the federal government may be done by the states through their state constitutions. States make laws about education, traffic, doctors, state lands, local government, criminals, state taxes, recreation, intrastate commerce, and in many other areas.

Each state has a government, much like the federal government. Each state has three branches of government with duties similar to those of the three branches of the federal government. Some exceptions would be foreign affairs, postal affairs, and defense, which are only the duties of the federal government.

State constitutions are much more detailed than the United States Constitution. For example, one state constitution is so comprehensive that it provides for the teaching of home economics in high schools. The United States Constitution leaves most of the details to Congress, but most states try to include all their details in writing. Because of this, state constitutions often get far behind the times, and many are in pressing need of revision.

Shared Powers

There are some areas over which state and federal governments both have power. For example, both can tax, borrow money, charter banks, establish courts, and encourage agriculture. These are the most important duties both share. Please refer to the chart on Page 27 for more details on shared powers.

QUESTIONS

TRUE OR FALSE? Write a *T* or *F* in the space provided.

____ 1. Under the full faith and credit clause, states do not have to accept the statutes of other states.

____ 2. Each state must treat the citizens of other states the same as it treats its citizens.

____ 3. States make laws about local government.

____ 4. The federal government must guarantee a republican form of government to the states.

____ 5. The 10th Amendment gives power to the people or states if not given to the federal government.

____ 6. State governments are similar to the federal government in that both have three branches.

____ 7. The format and wording of state constitutions are dictated by the federal government.

____ 8. The U.S. Constitution generally includes many more details than state constitutions.

FEDERAL OR STATE POWERS? Circle *federal* or *state* to indicate the body of government responsible.

1.	Provide education	*federal*	*state*
2.	Declare war	*federal*	*state*
3.	Print money	*federal*	*state*
4.	Issue a driver's license	*federal*	*state*
5.	Make treaties with other countries	*federal*	*state*
6.	Provide police and fire protection	*federal*	*state*
7.	Establish and operate post offices	*federal*	*state*

"The executive Power shall be vested in a President of the United States of America... during the Term of four Years, and, together with the Vice President, chosen for the same Term, be elected..." — United States Constitution, Article 2

The executive branch of government is established by Article 2 of the Constitution. The primary duty of the executive branch is to enforce or administer laws.

The President

President Joe Biden

The most prominent official in this branch is the president. The president and the vice president are the only national officers of the government elected by voters of the entire United States. The president faces critical issues daily. The day is long, and the pressures are enormous.

The president is thought of as being the representative of all the people. Unlike senators and representatives, all of the people in the United States vote for the president.

President Joe Biden took office in January 2021, after defeating Donald Trump in the 2020 presidential election. Per the 22nd Amendment, President Biden will be eligible to run again in the 2024 election, as he will have served only one of the two-term maximum.

Qualifications and Salary

The president and the vice president must be natural-born citizens, 35 years of age, and residents of the United States for at least 14 years.

The president and vice president must always be on the same party ticket. You vote for the president and the vice president at the same time, always assuring that the president and vice president are from the same political party.

The yearly salary of the president is $400,000, plus an expense allowance. The vice president receives a salary of $230,700, plus an expense allowance.

Before 1999, the president's salary had not been increased for more than 20 years. As a result, the pay was very low for the leader of the most powerful country in the world. Most chief executive officers of major American corporations make more than ten times the salary of the president. Finally, in 1999, Congress raised the president's salary from $200,000 to $400,000. If you adjust for inflation, the president today makes less than George Washington!

Oath of Office

Per the 20th Amendment, the first-term winner of the November presidential election assumes the duties of the office on January 20th. Before taking office, an oath must be performed.

The oath of office was established in the U.S. Constitution, Article 2, and is mandatory for a new or re-elected president. With the words of this simple oath, the president takes the most important political position in the world:

"I do solemnly swear (or affirm) that I will faithfully execute the Office of the President of the United States, and will to the best of my ability, preserve, protect and defend the Constitution of the United States."

The entire section of the Constitution that tells about the powers of the president contains only 320 words. Still, the wording is designed so that the office gets a maximum of inherent powers with necessary safeguards for the people.

The oath is typically administered by the Chief Justice of the Supreme Court. The ceremony takes place at the U.S. Capitol. After the oath, the president gives his or her *inaugural* speech. This tells the people the goals and direction of the nation. Over the years, this *Inauguration Day* has expanded from a simple ceremony to a day-long event, including parades, speeches, and balls.

The Vice President

Vice President Kamala Harris

Kamala Harris made history as the first woman elected vice president. The former U.S. senator from California is the 49th person to hold the office of vice president. The president assigns the vice president duties, and, in recent years, presidents have given considerable authority and responsibility to their vice presidents. The president needs support to ease the administrative burdens of the office. The vice president is also the president of the Senate and provides the president with a valuable link with Congress.

Vacancy

If the Office of the President becomes vacant, the vice president becomes president. Next in order of succession is the speaker of the House, then president pro tempore of the Senate, then members of the cabinet, starting with the secretary of state.

In 1973, the Office of the Vice President became vacant when Vice President Agnew resigned in a scandal. President Nixon made the first use of the 25th Amendment when he nominated Gerald Ford, House minority leader, as the new vice president. Congress approved the nomination. For more about the 25th Amendment, see Page 14.

Before 1974, the only way the Office of the President had become vacant was through death. However, in 1974, when President Nixon was involved in the Watergate cover-up, he became the first president ever to resign. Vice President Ford then became the 38th President of the United States.

Duties

In general, the duties of the president can be divided into five classes:

1. **Foreign Affairs** - The president makes treaties with Senate approval, nominates ambassadors and other foreign service officials, and receives diplomatic representatives. The president is in charge of all of our foreign affairs. Much of the work is done through one of the cabinet officials, the secretary of state.

2. **Domestic and Military Administration** - The president is the commander-in-chief of the armed forces, including state militia. Since the president appoints many domestic officials and prepares the nation's budget for congressional approval, the office has many national powers.

3. **Legislation** - The president may call both houses of Congress into *special session*. The president may recommend measures to Congress, and the president may veto bills from Congress. The president informs Congress on the progress of the nation and its needs through the "State of the Union" message at each session of Congress. As the political leader of the party in power, the president has much informal power over legislation.

4. **Appointment** - The president appoints a significant number of officials in the executive branch and the judicial branch. Some of these appointments include judges, cabinet members, advisors, department heads, etc. The Senate must approve many of these appointments.

5. **Judicial Functions** - The president may grant pardons and reprieves for federal offenses. An example of this was President Gerald Ford granting Richard Nixon a pardon for all federal crimes that he may have committed while serving as president.

Who Can Declare War?

Of the Constitution's many checks and balances, few have become as controversial as the country's war powers. As you have learned, the Constitution gives the power to declare war to the United States Congress in Article 1, section 8. It seems to be rather plainly stated that "The Congress shall have the power to declare war." But Article 2, section 2, names the president "Commander in Chief of the Army and Navy of the United States, and of the Militia of the several States, when called into actual Service of the United States." The president has often used his military powers to run a "war" that was never declared by Congress. So, it remains unclear precisely who can declare war. Congress has declared war on [11] occasions, and the president carries them out (i.e., World War I, World War II). Sometimes the president carries out a "war" that Congress does not want, as with the Vietnam War.

QUESTIONS

FILL IN THE BLANKS

1. What are the qualifications for president?_____
_____
2. What is the president's salary? _____
3. What are the five major areas of presidential duties?
_____
_____
_____
_____
_____
4. Who is the commander-in-chief of the armed forces?
_____
5. How long is the president's term?_____
6. What is the order of succession to the presidency?
_____
7. What is the main duty of the executive branch? _____
_____
8. Who is president?_____
9. Who is vice president? _____
10. Who is the head of the executive branch? _____
11. Name one president that has been impeached. _____
_____
12. Who is the only president ever to resign?_____

TRUE OR FALSE? Write a *T* or *F* in the space provided.

___ 1. The president can call both houses of Congress into special session.
___ 2. The president picks his successor.
___ 3. A presidential candidate is selected by Congress.
___ 4. The executive branch enforces our nation's laws.
___ 5. In 1973 when Vice President Agnew resigned, President Nixon designated his successor.
___ 6. Kamala Harris made history as the first woman elected vice president.
___ 7. The president and the vice president must be from the same political party.
___ 8. The president can make treaties without the approval of the Senate.
___ 9. The president cannot veto bills from Congress.
___ 10. The president may be re-elected three times.

MULTIPLE CHOICE - Circle the letter of the correct answer.

1. The national budget is presented by the:
   a. vice president **b.** secretary of state **c.** president
2. A salary of $230,700 is paid to:
   a. the president **b.** the vice president **c.** the cabinet
3. The president assumes the duties of office (after election) on: **a.** September 5 **b.** January 20 **c.** January 4
4. The executive branch is discussed in what article of the Constitution? **a.** 1   **b.** 2   **c.** 3   **d.** 4
5. The cabinet official involved with foreign affairs is the:
   a. secretary of state   **c.** vice president
   b. secretary of defense   **d.** attorney general
6. The 25th Amendment deals with what topic?
   a. abolishing slavery   **c.** voting rights
   b. vacancy of president   **d.** income tax

"...he (the President) may require the opinion, in writing, of the principal officer in each of the executive departments, upon any subject relating to the duties of their respective offices. . ." — U.S. Constitution, Article 2

The quote above is the closest mention the Constitution makes concerning the Cabinet. Those appointed by the president to these "executive departments" became known as members of the *President's Cabinet*. This group of presidential advisors now has 15 members, but President George Washington's first Cabinet had only four departments — State, War, Treasury, and Attorney General. Through the actions of succeeding presidents, cabinet officials were added to meet changing needs. Currently, cabinet members receive a salary of $199,700.

Here is a brief description of each department's work, the cabinet member's title, and the year the department was established.

The Department of State

The Secretary of State. This department is charged with foreign affairs, including participating in the United Nations, issuing passports, conducting negotiations, and running foreign embassies. (1789)

The Department of the Treasury

The Secretary of the Treasury. This department manages our nation's finances, is responsible for coining and printing of money, and enforces monetary laws. (1789)

The Department of the Interior

The Secretary of the Interior. This department is charged with all natural resources of the nation, scenic and historical regions, the National Parks System, Native American affairs, dams, and water power. (1849)

The Department of Agriculture

The Secretary of Agriculture. The USDA develops policy on farming, agriculture, and food. Its aims include assuring food safety, promoting agricultural trade and production, and ending hunger in America. (1862)

The Department of Justice

The Attorney General. This department enforces laws of the United States in federal courts, conducts suits in which the U.S. is concerned, and is the chief legal officer of the federal government. This department conducts investigations and lawsuits concerning monopolies, anti-trust laws, and organized crime. (1870)

The Department of Labor

The Secretary of Labor. This department protects workers' safety and wages, analyzes labor markets and trends, enforces labor laws, mediates strikes, and advance opportunities for employment. (1913)

The Department of Commerce

The Secretary of Commerce. This department is tasked with economic development by gathering data, issuing patents, utilizing innovative technology, and formulating business regulations. Also promotes exports and enforces trade agreements. (1913)

The Department of Defense

The Secretary of Defense. All provisions for the defense of the United States are carried out in this department, including the operation of the armed forces. (1949, originated in 1789 as the War Department.)

The Department of Housing and Urban Development

The Secretary of Housing and Urban Development. This department seeks solutions to the many problems of urban life. Its addition is an acknowledgment of the growing needs of urban living. (1965)

The Department of Transportation

The Secretary of Transportation. Transportation has become a vital problem for a complex society like ours. All methods and use of transportation come under this department's jurisdiction. The agencies at *DOT* promote safe and efficient travel, contributing to the nation's economic growth. (1966)

The Department of Energy

The Secretary of Energy. This agency establishes an energy policy for the U.S. It promotes the development of reliable, clean, and affordable energy. The DOE ensures nuclear security and protecting the environment. (1977)

The Department of Education

The Secretary of Education. This group manages all the federal education programs and offers monies to promote student achievement and equal access to all. (1979)

The Department of Health & Human Services

The Secretary of Health and Human Services. This department oversees health matters and many programs affecting the quality of American citizens' lives. Agencies include Public Health Service, Social Security, Food and Drug Administration, the Office of Vocational Rehabilitation, and many other programs affecting Americans of all ages. (1979)

The Department of Veterans Affairs

The Secretary of Veterans Affairs. This department administers benefit programs for veterans dealing with a broad range of issues from the country's wars and conflicts. Benefits include disability compensation, vocational rehabilitation, and medical care. (1989)

The Department of Homeland Security

The Secretary of Homeland Security. This is the latest cabinet addition deemed necessary because of the

continued

9/11 attacks and increased terrorism. The increasing threat of terrorist attacks made Americans realize a department like this is needed. This cabinet position oversees 240,000 workers from 22 agencies, including the Secret Service, border patrol, cybersecurity, and customs services. (2002)

In general, the secretaries play a significant role in advising the president in each of their areas. The secretaries are specialists in their field. The various cabinet members play a vital role in shaping national policy.

Executive Office of the President

Every day, the President of the United States is faced with scores of decisions, each with significant consequences for America's future. In addition to the cabinet, the president needs additional support to govern effectively. Thus, the *Executive Office of the President* (EOP) was created in 1939 by President Franklin D. Roosevelt. The EOP has responsibility for tasks ranging from communicating the president's message to the American people to promoting our trade interests abroad.

Executive Orders

Executive orders are controversial because they allow the president to make critical decisions, even law, without the consent of Congress. The U.S. Constitution does not explicitly mention executive orders. Still, presidents argue that the power to issue them is implied in the following statements in Article 2 of the Constitution: (1) "The executive power shall be vested in a President of the United States" and (2) "He shall take care that the laws be faithfully executed." Those who argue against or urge limits on the use of the unilateral power associated with executive orders remind us that the American system is based on the principle of checks and balances.

George Washington's first cabinet. It included a secretary of state (Thomas Jefferson), secretary of treasury (Alexander Hamilton), secretary of war (Henry Knox), and an attorney general (Edmund Randolph).

QUESTIONS

CABINET RESPONSIBILITIES. List which cabinet officer would be responsible for each of the following:

Social Security _____

Carrying out a war _____

Coining money_____

Enforcing U.S. laws in federal courts _____

Federal Railroad Administration _____

Foreign affairs _____

National parks _____

Farm programs_____

Settling a workers' strike _____

Constructing highways_____

Terrorism alerts _____

Benefits to military survivors_____

Renewable energy _____

Food and Drug Administration _____

Trade and export policies_____

Nuclear power production _____

Secret Service _____

Promotes workplace safety _____

Participation in the United Nations _____

Funding educational programs_____

TRUE OR FALSE? Write a *T* or *F* in the space provided.

___ 1. There were only three cabinet members in Washington's Cabinet.

___ 2. Cabinet members are part of the judicial branch.

___ 3. There are 12 cabinet positions today.

___ 4. The newest cabinet position is the Treasury Department.

___ 5. Cabinet members receive a salary of $109,000.

___ 6. After the president appoints a cabinet member, he or she must be approved by the Senate.

FILL IN THE BLANKS

1. Which cabinet position is headed by the attorney general? _____

2. The duties of the president and vice president are discussed in which article of the Constitution? _____

3. This cabinet position oversees the activities of the border patrol. _____

4. In addition to the Cabinet, what other office supports the many presidential activities? _____

5. Name the current Secretary of State._____

Perhaps the most prolonged debate at the Constitutional Convention concerned the method of selecting the president. An early suggestion was to give this power to Congress. But that would have destroyed the idea of the separation of powers. How could we have three branches of government, each checking the other if the legislative branch (the Congress) picked the head of the executive branch (the president)?

The writers of the Constitution also weren't ready to give the selection of the president to the people or the "common man." So they wrote a compromise into Article 2, Section 1 of the Constitution. The compromise set up a system of electors to select the president. These electors came to be known as the *Electoral College*, but the Constitution itself does not mention the term "Electoral College."

This unique election method was modified by the 12th and 23rd Amendments. Before 1961, the voters in Washington, D.C., didn't get to vote for the president at all. This was not considered fair in the capital of our country. The 23rd Amendment was added in 1961, giving three electoral votes for Washington, D.C. That made a total of 538 electors (electoral votes for each state equals the number of representatives plus two for the senators). A majority of 270 or more would be necessary to select the president. The map below shows the distribution of the electoral votes based on the 2010 reapportionment and will reflect additional changes from the 2020 census.

To summarize, if a candidate gets the most popular (people) votes in the state, the "electors" will then cast their votes the same way. All the electoral votes for the state (except for Maine and Nebraska) will go to the winner of the state. The writers of the Constitution also thought that the Electoral College gave states with a small population more equal weight in the presidential election.

One of the problems political scientists see in the Electoral College is that it allows a person to be elected president who has not won the popular vote in the country. In our growing beliefs in the power and rights of democracy in our nation, that could be a problem. Because all the electoral votes of a state go to the candidate who wins the election in that state, whether the candidate wins by a single vote or a million votes, it is possible to be elected president without having the most votes.

That has not happened very often, but it did occur in 2000 when George W. Bush became president and again recently in the 2016 election. Donald Trump became president even though Hillary Clinton won a majority of the popular votes. And, because this has happened so recently, Americans are debating the Electoral College's pros and cons. Since a change in the electoral vote would require a constitutional amendment, the change will not come quickly. Supporters of the current system say that it has served the nation well and forces candidates to gain broad geographic support rather than concentrating only on large metropolitan areas.

continued

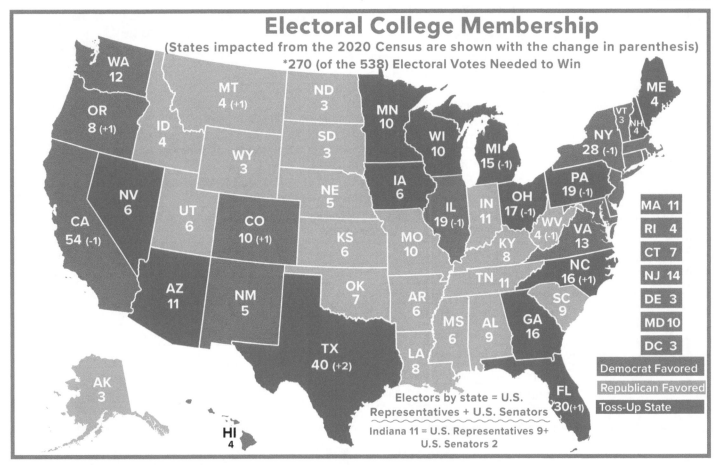

Electoral College Membership
(States impacted from the 2020 Census are shown with the change in parenthesis)
***270 (of the 538) Electoral Votes Needed to Win**

WA 12
OR 8 (+1)
MT 4 (+1)
ND 3
MN 10
ME 4
VT 3
NH 4
NY 28 (-1)
ID 4
SD 3
WI 10
MI 15 (-1)
NV 6
WY 3
IA 6
PA 19 (-1)
CA 54 (-1)
UT 6
CO 10 (+1)
NE 5
IL 19 (-1)
IN 11
OH 17 (-1)
WV 4 (-1)
VA 13
KS 6
MO 10
KY 8
NC 16 (+1)
AZ 11
NM 5
OK 7
AR 6
TN 11
SC 9
TX 40 (+2)
MS 6
AL 9
GA 16
LA 8
AK 3
FL 30 (+1)
HI 4

MA 11
RI 4
CT 7
NJ 14
DE 3
MD 10
DC 3

Democrat Favored
Republican Favored
Toss-Up State

Electors by state = U.S. Representatives + U.S. Senators

Indiana 11 = U.S. Representatives 9 + U.S. Senators 2

Political Party Symbols

In 1874, a political cartoonist, Thomas Nast, drew the Democrats as represented by a donkey, and the Republicans as represented by an elephant. The symbols stuck, and the parties themselves often use the symbols in advertising.

Elephant = Republican

Donkey = Democrat

QUESTIONS

TRUE OR FALSE? Write a **T** or **F** in the space provided.

___ 1. The term Electoral College comes from the Constitution itself.

___ 2. Although it was originally expected that a group of electors would actually elect the president and vice president, it became the practice for the electors to vote for the candidate who had the most popular votes.

___ 3. Popular vote means the vote of the people.

___ 4. There have been no elections in which the candidate with the most popular votes has not become president.

___ 5. The writers of the Constitution felt that the voters should directly elect the president and vice president.

___ 6. It would be easy to eliminate the Electoral College, only requiring the president's approval.

FILL IN THE BLANKS

1. How many electoral votes are there?_____

2. How many electoral votes for your state? _____

3. What is the minimum number of electoral votes for a state?_____

4. Which state has the most electoral votes?_____
_____

5. Name a president who was elected without winning the popular vote. _____

6. What political party does a donkey represent? _____

SHORT ANSWER

Should the Electoral College be abolished? Give an argument **for** or **against** this system. _____
_____
_____
_____

LEARNING AID — EXECUTIVE BRANCH FACT SHEET

Main Officers	The President and Vice President of the United States
Salaries	*The President:* $400,000 plus an expense allowance *The Vice President:* $230,700 plus an expense allowance *The Cabinet:* $199,700
Qualifications	The President and Vice President: 35 years old, a natural-born citizen, resident of the United States for 14 years
Terms of Office	Four years, may be re-elected once
Duties	Main duty of the executive branch is to enforce or administer laws. *The President:* controls foreign affairs and domestic powers, appoints many officials, grants pardons and reprieves, is commander-in-chief of the armed forces, prepares budget of the nation, is legislative leader of the political party in power. *The Vice President:* presides over the Senate of the United States, takes on duties assigned by the president, succeeds the Office of the President.
Advisors	*The Cabinet:* 15 department officials appointed by the president to aid in running our country. Department of: (along with key responsibility)

State: foreign affairs	*Health & Human Services:* health issues in U.S.
Justice: chief legal department	*Housing & Urban Development:* urban problems
Defense: defense of our country	*Transportation:* all domestic transportation
Interior: nation's natural resources	*Energy:* policies on energy, including conservation
Agriculture: farmers assistance, food inspection	*Education:* federal education matters
Labor: wage earners' assistance	*Veterans' Affairs:* matters that deal with veterans
Commerce: deals with business problems	*Homeland Security:* national security and war on terrorism
Treasury: nation's finances & coining of money	

Article Number	Article 2 of the U.S. Constitution

President Joe Biden is the 46th President of the United States. He is only the 45th person to serve as president; President Grover Cleveland served two nonconsecutive terms and thus is recognized as both the 22nd and the 24th president. Today, the president is limited to two four-year terms, but until the 22nd Amendment to the Constitution, ratified in 1951, a president could serve an unlimited number of terms. Franklin D. Roosevelt was elected president four times, serving from 1932 until his death in 1945; he is the only president ever to have served more than two terms.

Presidents of the United States

America's Founding Fathers decided that one elected civilian, the U.S. President, would lead the federal government's executive branch. This governmental structure has remained in place for more than 200 years. Here is the list of our nation's highest elected official.

	President	Term	Party
1.	George Washington	1789-1797	None
2.	John Adams	1797-1801	Federalist
3.	Thomas Jefferson	1801-1809	Dem.-Rep.
4.	James Madison	1809-1817	Dem.-Rep.
5.	James Monroe	1817-1825	Dem.-Rep.
6.	John Quincy Adams	1825-1829	Dem.-Rep.
7.	Andrew Jackson	1829-1837	Democrat
8.	Martin Van Buren	1837-1841	Democrat
9.	William H. Harrison	1841	Whig
10.	John Tyler	1841-1845	Whig
11.	James K. Polk	1845-1849	Democrat
12.	Zachary Taylor	1849-1850	Whig
13.	Millard Fillmore	1850-1853	Whig
14.	Franklin Pierce	1853-1857	Democrat
15.	James Buchanan	1857-1861	Democrat
16.	Abraham Lincoln	1861-1865	Republican
17.	Andrew Johnson	1865-1869	Democrat
18.	Ulysses S. Grant	1869-1877	Republican
19.	Rutherford B. Hayes	1877-1881	Republican
20.	James A. Garfield	1881	Republican
21.	Chester A. Arthur	1881-1885	Republican
22.	Grover Cleveland	1885-1889	Democrat
23.	Benjamin Harrison	1889-1893	Republican
24.	Grover Cleveland	1893-1897	Democrat
25.	William McKinley	1897-1901	Republican
26.	Theodore Roosevelt	1901-1909	Republican
27.	William H. Taft	1909-1913	Republican
28.	Woodrow Wilson	1913-1921	Democrat
29.	Warren G. Harding	1921-1923	Republican
30.	Calvin Coolidge	1923-1929	Republican
31.	Herbert Hoover	1929-1933	Republican
32.	Franklin D. Roosevelt	1933-1945	Democrat
33.	Harry S. Truman	1945-1953	Democrat
34.	Dwight D. Eisenhower	1953-1961	Republican
35.	John F. Kennedy	1961-1963	Democrat
36.	Lyndon B. Johnson	1963-1969	Democrat
37.	Richard M. Nixon	1969-1974	Republican
38.	Gerald R. Ford	1974-1977	Republican
39.	Jimmy Carter	1977-1981	Democrat
40.	Ronald Reagan	1981-1989	Republican
41.	George Bush	1989-1993	Republican
42.	William Clinton	1993-2001	Democrat
43.	George W. Bush	2001-2009	Republican
44.	Barack Obama	2009-2017	Democrat
45.	Donald Trump	2017-2021	Republican
46.	Joe Biden	2021-	Democrat

Women for President

Many women have sought to become President of the United States. A number received national attention, either as pioneers, potential candidates, or candidates of minor parties. However, none have been elected to the highest office. The 2020 presidential race started with six women seeking the Democratic nomination. However, none survived the primary elections.

Besides Hillary Clinton's recent runs, Victoria Woodhull became the first female presidential candidate in 1872. Shirley Chisholm sought the 1972 Democratic nomination, becoming the first black woman to run for president.

Frederick Douglass (1818-1895)

Born into slavery in Maryland, Frederick Douglass was a leader in the abolitionist movement and pushed for equality and human rights. He was the first African American citizen to hold a high U.S. government rank, advising presidents. In 1872 the Equal Rights Party's nominated Douglass to be Victoria Woodhull's running mate, which technically makes him the first Black vice presidential nominee. Years later, at the 1888 Republican National Convention, he received a vote for president.

QUESTIONS

FILL IN THE BLANKS

1. Which amendment limits the term of a president? ____

2. Which president was elected four times? _____
_____

3. What candidate ran for president even though they did not have the right to vote? _____

4. How many people have been president? _____

IDENTIFY THE PRESIDENTS. Mount Rushmore is a symbol of America, representing important events in the history of the United States. Who are the presidents?

1. _____   2. _____

3. _____   4. _____

If a 5th president was to be added, who would choose and why? _____
_____

Review of the 2020 Election

The 2020 presidential election featured the Republican incumbent, President Donald Trump, and former vice president, Democrat Joe Biden. Each political party accused the other of promoting unfair election tactics. Democrats urged voters to mail-in ballots and vote early, citing concerns over the coronavirus, changes at the United States Postal Service that could slow delivery, and long lines at voting locations. Republicans sought to limit the collection and counting of mail-in ballots, voicing concerns about the prospects for widespread voter fraud.

In the end, the 2020 election drew record turnout, with over 157 million Americans casting ballots. The election was contentious, fueling a turnout estimated to be the highest since 1900. Younger voters, ages 18 to 29, made their voices heard in historic numbers, and mail-in voting broke records in states around the nation, mostly because of health concerns over the pandemic. Battle lines were drawn over the handling of the COVID-19 outbreak and resulting economic fallout; national protests over racial inequity; the future of the Affordable Care Act; climate change; and Supreme Court nominees.

The country waited four days past Election Day to find out who had been elected to the president's office. President-elect Joe Biden was declared the winner, both in the popular vote and the Electoral College.

Candidate	Popular Vote	States	Electoral Votes
Biden	81,282,896	25 + DC	306
Trump	74,222,484	25	232

Democrat Favored | Republican Favored | "Swing" or Toss-Up

◯ = Biden won

Threats to Our Democracy

The 2020 election saw unprecedented attacks seeking to undermine public confidence in our elections:

- voters fearing violence during or after the election;
- citizens concerned their votes would not be counted;
- politicians attempting to prevent votes from being counted;
- disinformation campaigns on social media;
- efforts to convince state legislatures to ignore the popular vote and;
- the concern for a peaceful transfer of power.

These are all threats to our democracy, and our leaders and citizens must work to bring the country together. A democracy cannot function long under those conditions. With the lessons of 2020, both political parties and all levels of government will take action to defend our democracy.

Are Elections Secure?

In the end, the result was that our elections are secure. That was the conclusion of the *Department of Justice*, the *Department of Homeland Security*, and election officials of both parties in crucial battleground states. More than two dozen lawsuits filed by President Trump's legal team were dismissed either by federal or state judges. Each state certified their election results followed by the Electoral College's official votes, leading to 306 electoral votes (270 needed to win) for Joe Biden.

Every Vote Counts

More and more, we see election results with razor-thin margins. Even with long lines for voters, it was heartening to see so many millions of Americans determined to exercise their constitutional right to cast a ballot. The record-breaking turnout reaffirmed that voting is a right Americans are no longer taking for granted.

The U.S. does not have a national election system by design. The 2020 election illustrated different rules and regulations across 10,000 election jurisdictions. Our representatives will need to explore more uniform federal election standards that could simplify matters for voters, especially on voter registration, early voting, and access to by-mail voting. The challenge is to do this without conflicting with the 10th Amendment and the right of states to administer elections in the manner they choose.

QUESTIONS

TRUE OR FALSE? Write a *T* or *F* in the space provided.

_____ 1. Joe Biden won the electoral vote, but lost the popular vote.

_____ 2. The 2020 election had the largest turnout since 1900.

_____ 3. The election results took several days to become official due to the large number of mail-in votes.

_____ 4. The federal government sets strict standards on how each state conducts elections.

_____ 5. Each state certifies their election results.

SHORT ANSWER - REFER TO ELECTION MAP

1. Which party dominates which region? _____

_____

2. Which party is favored in rural areas? _____

3. Which party is favored in urban areas? _____

4. Define "swing states" and give an example. _____

_____

_____

"The judicial power of the United States, shall be vested in one supreme court, and in such inferior courts..."
—— United States Constitution, Article 3, Section 1

The main purpose of the judicial branch is to interpret the laws and administer justice. Many of the details of this branch may be found in Article 3 of the Constitution. The judicial branch consists of a system of federal courts.

While the people elect the executive and legislative branches, the judicial branch is appointed by the president and confirmed by the Senate. Each federal judge holds office for life and may be removed only by impeachment. There are no expressed qualifications for federal judges in the Constitution.

Power of the Judicial Branch

The power of the judicial branch through the courts is extended to all cases arising under the Constitution, laws, and treaties of the United States and in some other special circumstances (see Article 3, Section 2). Every person accused of wrongdoing has the right to a fair trial before a competent judge and a jury of one's peers.

Under the Constitution, the courts protect the rights of all citizens and guarantee justice based on law. The philosophy of our law (often referred to as *jurisprudence*) relies heavily on past precedent. Courts will review cases that were previously decided when analyzing a new case brought to the courts. The decision of similar cases will mostly be the same as courts utilize this past precedent.

Most court cases fall into two categories, *criminal* or *civil* cases. Most crimes are a violation of state law, not federal law, and would be prosecuted in the state court system. Only crimes that break a law of the U.S. government will be prosecuted in the federal courts.

In criminal cases, the court decides if an accused person is guilty or innocent of a crime. Examples of federal crimes include bank robbery, counterfeiting, kidnapping, and financial fraud. In civil cases, the court settles disputes between two parties. Civil cases that may be heard in federal court include questions over national law, suing for civil rights and first amendment violations, and resolving disputes (over $75,000) between parties from different states.

There are three major types of federal courts in the U.S. court system::

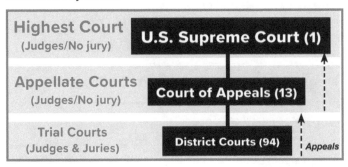

The Supreme Court

"Equal Justice Under Law" - These words, written above the main entrance to the Supreme Court Building, express the ultimate responsibility of the Supreme Court of the United States. The unique position of the Supreme Court is the result of the strong commitment of the American people to the *Rule of Law* and constitutional government. The Supreme Court ensures democracy and the importance of the oldest written Constitution still in force.

A primary duty of the *justices* (judges) of the Supreme Court is to decide whether state and federal laws are constitutional and whether actions by lower courts or other governmental agencies are lawful. This power is not given to the Supreme Court directly by the Constitution, but precedence and tradition have given the court this power.

Parties who are not satisfied with the decision of a lower court must petition the Supreme Court. The petition is called a *writ of certiorari*. This requests a lower court to submit the record of the case for review. Typically, the Courts hear cases of appeal from the U.S. Court of Appeals or the highest court in a given state. In some exceptional cases, the Court hears the issue directly. The Supreme Court accepts around 100 of the more than 7,000 cases that it is asked to review each year.

There are nine Supreme Court justices with one justice serving as *chief justice*. The Constitution does not stipulate the number of Supreme Court justices; the number is set instead by Congress. Court justices receive a salary of $213,900. The chief justice receives a salary of $223,500. A quorum of six Justices is required to decide a case, and a majority is necessary for a decision. The court meets in the U.S. Supreme Court Building in Washington, D.C. Typically, the court conducts its annual term from the first Monday of October until late June the following year.

In April 2022, the Senate confirmed Judge Ketanji Brown Jackson, becoming the first Black woman to serve on the nation's highest court. Jackson was nominated by President Biden and will replace the retiring Justice, Stephen Breyer.

	Supreme Court Justice	Type of Justice	President Who Nominated
1.	John Roberts, Jr.	Chief Justice	G.W. Bush (R)
2.	Clarence Thomas	Associate Justice	G.H. Bush (R)
3.	Ketanji B. Jackson	Associate Justice	Biden (D)
4.	Samuel A. Alito Jr.	Associate Justice	G.W. Bush (R)
5.	Sonia M. Sotomayor	Associate Justice	Obama (D)
6.	Elena Kagan	Associate Justice	Obama (D)
7.	Neil Gorsuch	Associate Justice	Trump (R)
8.	Brett M. Kavanaugh	Associate Justice	Trump (R)
9.	Amy Coney Barrett	Associate Justice	Trump (R)

Court of Appeals

The United States has 13 *courts of appeal*, one court in each of the 12 federal circuits that divide the country and one *Court of Appeals for the Federal Circuit* which has nationwide jurisdiction to hear appeals in specialized cases.

Their primary job is to hear cases of appeal from lower courts and determine whether the law was applied correctly. The appellate courts do not retry cases or hear new evidence. They do not hear witnesses testify. Appeals courts consist of three or more judges and do not use a jury. These judges are appointed for life by the president and confirmed by the Senate.

These courts were created in 1891 to relieve the Supreme Court of the significant burden of cases appealed from the district courts. As we previously learned, the Supreme Court hears only a small number of cases. That means the decisions made by the 12 Circuit Courts of Appeals across the country and the Federal Circuit Court are the last word in thousands of cases.

District Courts

There are 94 *district courts* in the United States. Most people would come in contact with a U.S. District Court if they were involved in a federal legal issue. The district courts are the ordinary trial courts in the federal system. Almost all cases heard in the federal system begin here.

Each court has one to 24 judges. Trial courts include the district judge who tries the case and a jury that decides the case. Each district court judge is appointed by the president and confirmed by the Senate for a life term.

There is at least one district court in each state and the District of Columbia. Each district includes a U.S. bankruptcy court as a unit of the district court. Four territories of the United States have U.S. district courts that hear federal cases, including bankruptcy cases: Puerto Rico, the Virgin Islands, Guam, and the Northern Mariana Islands.

There are other courts for special cases, having national jurisdiction. The *Court of International Trade* addresses cases involving international trade and customs laws. The *U.S. Court of Federal Claims* deals with most claims for money damages against the U.S. government. The *United States Tax Court* is a court in Washington, D.C. created as an independent judicial authority for citizens disputing specific tax issues. As their names show, their duties are limited to specific areas. Also, states have court systems for state matters.

Rule of Law

President Theodore Roosevelt once said, "Ours is a government of liberty, by, through and under the law. No man is above it, and no man is below it." The *rule of law* is a principle under which no person or group, including the government and its leaders, is above the law. This includes the following principles:

- The same laws govern every citizen
- Everyone's rights are respected
- Laws protect our fundamental rights
- Because people make laws through their elected representatives, people are willing to obey these laws

In the United States, we have written rules to help us settle disagreements peacefully through a fair system of justice. It is the job of the courts to interpret the laws. It is up to judges and juries to decide if we have indeed broken the law.

QUESTIONS

WHICH COURT? Which federal court fits the statement given? Answer *Supreme Court (**SC**)*, *Court of Appeals (**CA**)*, *District Court (**DC**)*, *none (**N**)*, or *all (**A**)*.

____ 1. This court could declare the final word on the constitutionality of a state law.
____ 2. This court could declare the final word on the constitutionality of a federal law.
____ 3. Judges are appointed.
____ 4. Judges serve for life.
____ 5. This court has nine judges.
____ 6. The judges are removed only by impeachment.
____ 7. Ordinary trial courts of the federal system.
____ 8. Has 13 courts.
____ 9. Meets in its own building in Washington, D.C.
____ 10. The judges must be 32 years or older.
____ 11. This court has a chief justice as head officer.
____ 12. Most court cases begin here.
____ 13. Courts that are described in Article 3 of the Constitution.
____ 14. Appointment approved by the Senate.
____ 15. Salary of $173,600.
____ 16. Elected by the people.
____ 17. Judges must be natural-born citizens.
____ 18. Appointed by the president.
____ 19. Judges must have law degrees.
____ 20. Judges serve without salary.

FILL IN THE BLANKS

1. Who appoints Supreme Court judges? _____
2. Who must approve Supreme Court appointments? _____
3. Who is the current chief justice of the Supreme Court? _____
4. What is a *civil* case? _____

Give one example. _____

"Laws are a dead letter without courts to expound their true meaning and operation." – Alexander Hamilton

Judicial review is the name given to the process by which the courts interpret the meaning of the Constitution and the laws passed under it. It is clear that the Constitution is the supreme law of our land and takes precedence over any law passed or any action taken by any state or federal official.

However, the Constitution is not a complete legal code, and it is not always easy to see how the Constitution can be applied to particular cases. As conditions change, new interpretations may be placed on the Constitution; actions may be taken in areas not directly covered by the Constitution.

Someone, then, must have the authority to precisely decide what the Constitution means and decide if the government is acting within constitutional limits. Most historians agree that the Constitutional Convention members wanted the courts to have the power of judicial review, even though they did not write it out in detail. They thought that the idea had been conveyed adequately through the wording of Article 3, the judicial article, and Article 6, the "supreme law of the land" clause.

There was some discussion of this question after the Constitutional Convention. Still, nothing was settled until 1803, when the Supreme Court handed down its decision in the case of *Marbury v. Madison*. The court ruled that one section of a 1789 law was contrary to the Constitution and, therefore, was not valid.

"It is emphatically the province and duty of the Judicial Department to say what the law is...If two laws conflict with each other, the Courts must decide on the operation of each. So, if a law be in opposition to the Constitution... the Court must determine which of these conflicting rules governs the case. This is of the very essence of judicial duty."

The above ruling from *Marbury v. Madison* established the precedent for judicial review, an essential addition to the system of checks and balances to prevent any one branch of the government from becoming too powerful. Judicial review in the United States has been a model for other countries.

Cases Handled by the Federal Courts

The federal courts are often called the "guardians of the Constitution" because their rulings protect rights and liberties guaranteed by the Constitution. Through fair and impartial judgments, the federal courts interpret and apply the law to resolve disputes. An important distinction should be noted: Courts do not make the laws; that is the responsibility of Congress. The subjects of Judicial Review also include the legislative actions from Congress, the executive actions from the president and government agencies, and state and local laws.

On the next page, you will find examples of cases that are handled by the federal court system.

continued

LEARNING AID	**JUDICIAL BRANCH FACT SHEET**
Main Courts	*The Supreme Court, Court of Appeals,* and *District Courts.*
Number of Courts	*Supreme Court:* 1 *Court of Appeals*: 13 *District Courts*: 94
Number of Judges	*Supreme Court:* 9 *Court of Appeals:* 3 to 9 *District Courts:* 1 to 24
Supreme Court Salaries	$223,500 for Supreme Court chief justice $213,900 for Supreme Court associate justices
Terms of Office	For life; may be removed only by impeachment.
Duties	Main duty of the judicial branch is to interpret laws and administer justice. *Supreme Court:* Decide if laws are constitutional *Court of Appeals:* Hear appeals from lower courts *District Courts:* Ordinary trial courts, federal cases begin here Other courts handle special cases, examples include U.S. Claims Court and U.S. Tax Court.
Meeting Place	*Supreme Court:* Washington, D.C. *Court of Appeals:* various circuits *District Courts:* various districts
Article Number in Constitution	Article 3 of the U.S. Constitution

The United States Federal Courts

Cases Involving:	Examples of such cases:
Constitution of the U.S.	Freedoms in the Bill of Rights
Federal Laws and Regulations	Taxes, Social Security, civil rights, environment violations
Disputes Between States	Environmental issues including water rights and pollution
International Trade Laws	Flow of goods among countries
Disputes between parties in different states	Lawsuits involving people and companies that do business in different states
Patent, Copyright, and Intellectual Property Laws	Exclusive rights and compensation for creative work and inventions
Habeas Corpus Petitions	Court review of jailed person's claim of unlawful imprisonment

The Supreme Court's right to interpret the Constit-ution has been challenged at times but has always been upheld. In a sense, all of our courts contribute to the Constitution's interpretation through the rulings they hand down on various cases involving the Constitution. The Supreme Court has used its power of judicial review to overturn more than a hundred acts of Congress and more than a thousand state laws. Also, the Supreme Court can and often does overturn the rulings of lower courts. It is the final authority on the meaning of the Constitution.

Landmark Supreme Court Cases

Besides the case of *Marbury v. Madison* (discussed on the previous page) there have been several other important Supreme Court cases. As you have learned, the nine Supreme Court justices exert a powerful influence over the course of the nation and the lives of Americans. Here is a sampling of such cases:

- *McCulloch v. Maryland* (1819): Established the constitutional supremacy of the federal government over state government.
- *Dred Scott v. Sanford* (1857): Declared the Missouri Compromise unconstitutional; it also determined that slaves were not citizens of the United States.
- *Ableman v. Booth* (1859): The U.S. Supreme Court denied state courts the right to issue rulings that conflicted with the decisions of federal courts; helped interpret federalism.
- *Plessy v. Ferguson* (1896): Ruled that separate but equal facilities for blacks and whites on trains did not violate civil rights of blacks. This "separate but equal" doctrine remained valid until the Brown v. Board of Education decision in 1954.
- *Schenck v. U.S.* (1919): Declared that the United States government can restrict free speech "if the words used... create a clear and present danger."

- *Gitlow v. New York* (1925): Decision confirmed that the Bill of Rights applies to the states.
- *Schechter v. U.S.* (1935): Ruled that Congress cannot delegate its power and authority to the president.
- *Brown v. Board of Education* (1954): Laws enforcing segregation in schools are unconstitutional, violating the equal protection guarantee of the 14th Amendment.
- *Miranda v. Arizona* (1966): Ruled that suspects of a crime must be informed of their rights.
- *U.S. Term Limits Inc. v. Thorton* (1995): Ruled that neither the states nor Congress could limit terms of the members of Congress.
- *District of Columbia v. Heller* (2008): protects the right to keep a handgun in his home for purposes of self-defense.
- *Roe v. Wade* overturned (2022): The Supreme Court overturned by a 5-4 majority *Roe v. Wade*, the court's landmark 1973 judgment that made abortion a constitutional right. The overturning of *Roe* leaves abortion laws entirely up to the states.

Student Rights and the Constitution

The Supreme Court has ruled on cases involving young people under the age of 18. Although many of you are not old enough to vote, this does not prevent you from enjoying the same fundamental constitutional rights as adults.

The Constitution applies to all, including students' rights, but does acknowledge that there must be considerations for age and maturity levels. The rights of free speech, free press, and freedom from unwarranted search and seizure have been debated by parents, students, and school administrators for many decades.

QUESTIONS

FILL IN THE BLANKS

1. This name is given to the process by which courts interpret the meaning of the Constitution and the laws passed under it. _____

2. What article in the Constitution discusses the judicial branch? _____

3. What important case came before the Supreme Court in 1803?_____

4. What court is the final authority on the meaning of the Constitution? _____

5. What is the salary of the Chief Justice? _____

TRUE OR FALSE? Write a *T* or *F* in the space provided.

___ 1. The Constitution has no impact on teenagers.
___ 2. Landmark cases help predict the decisions of current judicial cases.
___ 3. The Constitution is always easily interpreted.
___ 4. The ruling in the case of *Plessy v. Ferguson* was overturned in 1954.
___ 5. Several Supreme Court decisions have been overturned by the President of the United States.
___ 6. The First Amendment allows for the freedom of religion, speech, press, assembly, and petition.
___ 7. The Federal Courts would rule on cases involving international trade.

The authors of the Constitution wanted to be sure that no person or group would seize power and control the American government. To ensure that this would not happen, our United States government was divided into three parts: the executive, the legislative, and the judicial under the Constitution. Each of these three branches has a check on the powers of the others. These checks provide a system of balance in our government, which is why we call the system *checks and balances*.

You may also hear this system referred to as a *separation of powers*. Although not directly mentioned in the Constitution, the first three articles mark the executive, legislative, and judicial responsibilities. It gives some power to each branch of government instead of giving all the power to one branch.

These are the most important checks and balances:

1. *Executive branch* has the power to check the legislative branch by vetoing laws that Congress wants to pass.

2. *Legislative branch* may check the executive branch by passing laws over the veto by a two-thirds vote in each house.

3. *Judicial branch* may check both the legislative and executive by declaring laws unconstitutional.

Obviously, this is not the whole system, but it is the main idea. Other checks and balances include:

Executive over the judicial branch: The president appoints all federal judges and may grant pardons or reprieves for those convicted in court.

Legislative over the executive branch: The legislative branch must approve appointments that the president makes; the Senate must approve treaties that the president makes, and the legislative branch may investigate the executive branch.

Legislative over the judicial branch: The legislative branch must approve the president's choice of judges to the judicial branch and may propose constitutional amendments to overturn judicial decisions.

Legislative over the executive and judicial branch: The legislative branch has impeachment powers over federal officers.

Judicial over the executive branch: The president cannot fire or remove Supreme Court justices.

There are other checks and balances in the American government besides those between branches of government. They include:

Checks in Congress

The Senate and House can check each other by rejecting bills passed by the other. The House has the added check of sole power to start revenue bills.

continued

A System of Checks and Balances

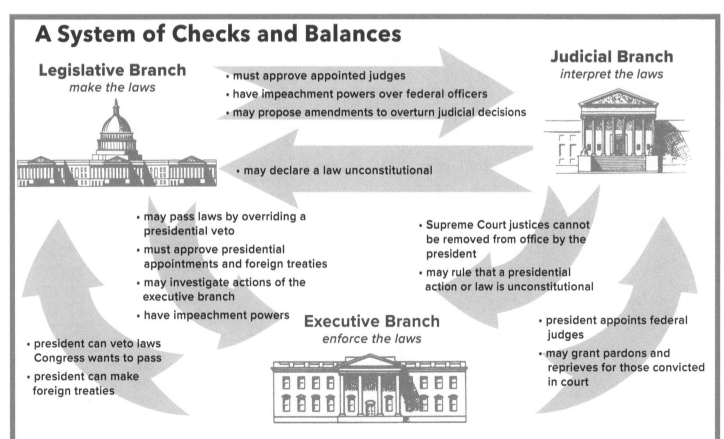

Legislative Branch
make the laws

Judicial Branch
interpret the laws

- must approve appointed judges
- have impeachment powers over federal officers
- may propose amendments to overturn judicial decisions

- may declare a law unconstitutional

- may pass laws by overriding a presidential veto
- must approve presidential appointments and foreign treaties
- may investigate actions of the executive branch
- have impeachment powers

- Supreme Court justices cannot be removed from office by the president
- may rule that a presidential action or law is unconstitutional

- president can veto laws Congress wants to pass
- president can make foreign treaties

Executive Branch
enforce the laws

- president appoints federal judges
- may grant pardons and reprieves for those convicted in court

Checks on the People

A president is not elected directly by the people; only one-third of the Senate is elected at one time; and judges are not elected by the people.

Power to the People

The Declaration of Independence is a clear statement of the American belief that government must serve the people and not the other way around. These ideas guided the writing of the Constitution and the first three words, "**We the People**..." This protects the people from a too-powerful government and grants you select powers. You have the right to elect government members and limit how long government leaders can be in office.

The power to govern belongs to the people (either directly or through representation) is called *popular sovereignty*. The government can only function with the consent of the people.

In addition to the federal government, most state and local governments have the mechanics of a system of checks and balances.

Federalism

Another check and balance is the theory of *federalism*, or the sharing of power between the federal, state, and local governments. In many ways, this is a natural division of functions. Local governments handle local affairs; national affairs by the federal government.

While each of the 50 states has its own constitution, all provisions for state constitutions must comply with the U.S. Constitution. For example, a state constitution cannot deny accused criminals the right to a trial by jury, as assured by the U.S. Constitution's Sixth Amendment.

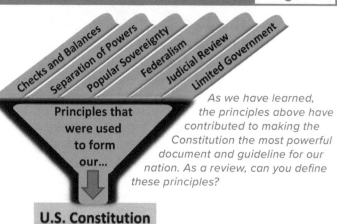

As we have learned, the principles above have contributed to making the Constitution the most powerful document and guideline for our nation. As a review, can you define these principles?

QUESTIONS

1. Why is there a system of checks and balances?

_____

_____

2. Name the three branches of the federal government.

_____

_____

TRUE OR FALSE? Write a ***T*** or ***F*** in the space provided.

____ 1. The judicial branch has no check on the other branches.

____ 2. State constitutions do not need to comply with the U.S. Constitution.

____ 3. The theory of federalism is a division of power between the states and federal government.

____ 4. There are checks on the people, too.

____ 5. The Supreme Court judges are appointed by Congress.

____ 6. Once a Supreme Court judge is appointed, he/she may never be removed.

____ 7. The president's veto is part of the system of checks and balances.

____ 8. The power to govern belonging to the people is called popular sovereignty.

____ 9. George Washington was known as the Father of the Constitution.

____ 10. The legislative branch has impeachment powers.

FILL IN THE BOXES (CHECKS & BALANCES)

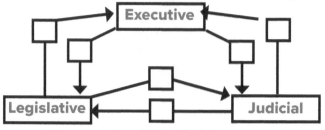

a. president appoints federal judges
b. must approve appointed judges
c. may pass laws by overriding a veto
d. may declare laws from Congress unconstitutional
e. may veto laws passed by Congress
f. Supreme Court justices may not be fired

James Madison
Fight for Checks and Balances

Known as the "Father of the Constitution," James Madison campaigned vigorously for a system of checks and balances in the governmental framework. In the "Federalists Papers," Madison wrote extensively on this balance of power and how this would control the interests of various groups. Madison argued that the larger the society, and the more diverse interests of its citizens, the more likely each faction would be to thwart the interests of other factions seeking control. These concepts helped lead to the success of the Constitution and its ultimate ratification.

Our constitutional form of government can be changed without revolution or rebellion. The authors of the Constitution, revolutionaries themselves, felt there should be provisions for orderly change.

The amendment process is discussed in Article 5 of the Constitution. To make an amendment to the Constitution, the amendment must be proposed by either the states or Congress and then ratified by the states. Here is a summary of the details:

AMENDING THE CONSTITUTION

Methods of Proposing Constitutional Amendments

By Congress with a two-thirds vote of both houses.

or

By national convention called by Congress at the request of two-thirds (34) of the state legislatures.

Methods of Ratifying Constitutional Amendments

By state legislatures in three-fourths (38) of the states.

or

By state conventions in three-fourths (38) of the states.

Proposing Amendments

There are two methods of proposing amendments to the Constitution:

1. Congress may propose amendments approved by a two-thirds majority in each house, or

2. The legislatures of two-thirds of the states may require Congress to summon a constitutional convention to consider amendments.

Ratifying Amendments

There are two ways of ratifying amendments to the Constitution:

1. An amendment is official when three-fourths of state legislatures approve it, or

2. When special conventions in three-fourths of the states approve it.

Every amendment except the 21st was approved by using the first method of proposing and ratifying.

Miscellaneous Constitutional Information

In Article 4 of the Constitution, debts made under the Articles of Confederation were declared valid under the new government of the Constitution.

Article 6 of the Constitution lists no religious tests for government office. John F. Kennedy was the first Catholic to be elected president, and there has never been a Jewish president. Article 6 requires government officials to take an oath supporting the Constitution.

Amendments to the United States Constitution may be adopted whenever the need arises. The 16th Amendment was passed to allow income taxes after an earlier income tax law was unconstitutional by the U.S. Supreme Court. This is not to say that the U.S. Constitution is changed without much thought and consideration. Since the adoption of the U.S. Constitution in the late 1700s, there have only been 27 amendments. By comparison, Alabama has 799 amendments to its state constitution, which is over 100 years old.

To repeal an existing amendment, there must be another amendment added. There has been only one amendment repealed, the 18th (prohibition). The 18th Amendment will remain in the Constitution, but a notation has been added to mention that this has been repealed by the 21st.

Amendments are Rarely Ratified

Thousands of amendments have been proposed since the Constitution was written, but only 27 have been ratified. Below are examples of failed amendments:

- Changing the voting age to 16
- Eliminating income tax
- Making English the official language
- Providing moments of silence in schools
- Desecrating the American flag is illegal

What do you think will be the next topic that becomes our 28th Amendment?

QUESTIONS

1. Describe the most common process used in amending the Constitution. _____

_____

_____

2. Does the Constitution outline religious qualifications for the president? _____

3. How many states does it take to ratify an amendment?

_____

4. What is stated in the 16th Amendment? _____

_____

_____

5. How many amendments to the Constitution have been made? _____

6. Which article of the Constitution describes the amending process? _____

7. When was the last amendment passed and what was the topic? _____

_____

On June 14, 1777, less than a year after the Declaration of Independence was signed, the Continental Congress adopted the *Stars and Stripes* as the flag of the United States. Original plans to provide a  new star and a new stripe for each new state proved impractical, and it was decided that only a new star would be added with each new state. Today, our flag retains 13 stripes in honor of the 13 original colonies and 50 stars, one for each of the 50 states.

We look upon our flag as a symbol of union, freedom, and justice. Historically, the red of the flag stands for courage, the white for liberty, the blue for loyalty. The number of stars shows our nation's growth, and the flag is not only an emblem but a history of our country, as well.

It should be important to all Americans to fly the flag from their homes on national holidays and other patriotic occasions. When we pledge allegiance to our flag, it is not a pledge to any person or political party, but the United States Constitution and its ideals.

When the flag passes in a parade or during the ceremony of raising or lowering the flag, all persons present should face the flag, stand at attention and salute, and men should remove their hats.

The Pledge of Allegiance

Thirty-one words that affirm the values and freedom the American flag represents are recited while facing the flag as a pledge of Americans' loyalty to their country.

"I pledge allegiance to the flag of the United States of America, and to the Republic for which it stands, one nation under God, indivisible, with liberty and justice for all."

Flag Code Rules

All Americans should treat the country's flag with respect and follow established conduct in the use and display. Some of the main points of the flag code are shown here. Consult a copy of the complete code, found in your library or on the internet, when you have other questions about the flag.

- The flag should be flown only from sunrise to sunset.
- The flag should be hoisted briskly and lowered ceremoniously.
- When displayed against the wall, the union should be on top and to the flag's right, your left.
- The flag may be used to cover a casket, but should not be lowered into the ground.
- In a procession, the flag should always be in the front.
- When shown with flags of states or other groups, the flag should be in the center and highest.

- When shown with flags of other nations, the American flag should not be flown higher than others.
- The flag should never be used as a cover.
- The flag should be displayed daily and especially on national holidays.
- The exact likeness of the flag should never be used for advertising.
- Nothing should be attached to the flag.
- The flag should never be allowed to touch the ground or floor, not be used as a carrying device, nor brush against any objects, nor be used as a drapery of any sort.
- Worn flags should be burned and not thrown in the trash.
- On a speaker's platform, the flag should be displayed at the right if it is on a staff or on the wall behind the speaker if it is flat.
- Flags flown from fixed staffs are placed at half staff to indicate mourning. The flag so used should be first raised to the peak and then lowered to half-staff; it is again raised to the peak before lowering.

Contrary to popular belief, the flag code is not a law with penalties. It is a guide for American citizens on the best etiquette for displaying and honoring the American flag. The Supreme Court has ruled that even those who desecrate the flag by burning or mutilating the flag are merely exercising their rights of free speech and cannot be prosecuted. However, most Americans heed the flag code and treat it very seriously.

From our independence in 1776 until today, many Americans have fought for and died to preserve the ideals of democracy represented by the flag.

Who Designed the Flag?

Did Betsy Ross design the flag? Probably not. Historians have been unable to find solid evidence that Betsy was involved in either making or designing the flag. Best guess as who did? Probably Francis Hopkinson, a naval flag designer, who billed Congress for that service in 1781.

QUESTIONS

1. What do the stars of the flag stand for? _____
2. What do the stripes of the flag stand for? _____
3. What does the red of the flag stand for? _____
4. What does the blue of the flag stand for? _____

TRUE OR FALSE? Write a *T* or *F* in the space provided.

___ 1. Worn flags should be burned, not put in the trash.

___ 2. The flag should be used to advertise only if the products advertised are in good taste.

___ 3. The flag should be in the rear of a procession and centered.

___ 4. The flag should be flown only on holidays.

___ 5. The flag can be displayed on public buildings.

The Congress, shall have the power to lay and collect taxes..., to pay the debts..., to borrow money..., to coin money..."
—U.S. Constitution, Article 1, Section 8

The Constitution gives Congress the power to manage spending of the federal government. Since Congress must decide how the government will spend money, it makes a budget each year.

The *budget* is the federal government's plan for raising and spending money for a year. Both the executive branch (the president) and the legislative branch (the Congress) get involved. The government's taxing and spending policies are called *fiscal policies*.

While Congress has control over federal taxing and spending, laws passed since 1921 have given the president the responsibility of preparing an annual budget that must be ready in January of each year. This budget is then presented to Congress. Congress then debates possible changes or additions. The houses make numerous changes, but their work must be done by October. The *fiscal year* begins October 1st and ends on September 30th. An example is Fiscal Year 2023, which starts on October 1, 2022, and ends on September 30, 2023.

The best way for a student to study the federal budget quickly is to look at the annual budget graph. This graph is typical of many of the yearly budgets of the past few years. It will give you a quick idea of where the federal government gets its money and where it spends it.

With a government budget now $4.8 trillion, it is easy to see how government shapes American economics. Economics is the study of how people and countries use their resources to produce, distribute, and consume goods and services. When the government spends its trillion dollars, it affects jobs, businesses, farms, and families. When the government borrows, it affects banks and all those who might also borrow money. When government taxes, it affects how much people will have left to take care of their families. While government activity is not the only factor in the American economy, it is an important one.

How Much Is The National Debt?

$1	one
$10	ten
$100	one hundred
$1,000	one thousand
$10,000	ten thousand
$100,000	one hundred thousand
$1,000,000	one million
$10,000,000	ten million
$100,000,000	one hundred million
$1,000,000,000	one billion
$10,000,000,000	ten billion
$100,000,000,000	one hundred billion
$1,000,000,000,000	one trillion
$10,000,000,000,000	ten trillion
$30,000,000,000,000	NATIONAL DEBT

*If you divided the national debt by the number of people in the United States, each man, woman, and child would owe more than $91,000.

QUESTIONS

FILL IN THE BLANKS

1. The Constitution gives the power to manage the spending of the federal government to what body?

_____

2. The federal government's plan for raising money and spending for a year is called the _____ .

3. Who prepares the annual budget and then presents it to Congress in January of each year? _____

4. What taxes provide the federal government with most of its money? *(see chart below)*

_____

5. What month does the fiscal year begin? _____

6. Indicate how much the government spends on the following *(approximate percentage, see chart below)*:

   Medicare and Health_____

   National Defense _____

   Social Security, Unemployment, & Labor _____

   Interest on Debt _____

RECENT FEDERAL GOVERNMENT RECEIPTS & SPENDING (annually)

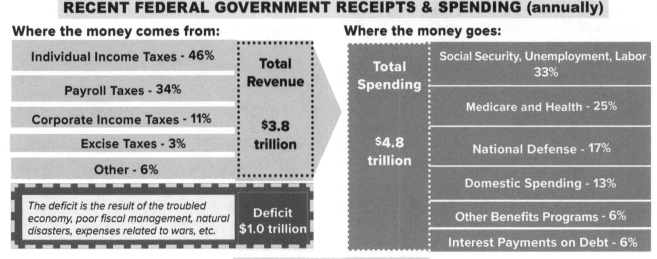

Where the money comes from:

- Individual Income Taxes - 46%
- Payroll Taxes - 34%
- Corporate Income Taxes - 11%
- Excise Taxes - 3%
- Other - 6%

Total Revenue

$3.8 trillion

The deficit is the result of the troubled economy, poor fiscal management, natural disasters, expenses related to wars, etc.

Deficit $1.0 trillion

Where the money goes:

Total Spending

$4.8 trillion

- Social Security, Unemployment, Labor - 33%
- Medicare and Health - 25%
- National Defense - 17%
- Domestic Spending - 13%
- Other Benefits Programs - 6%
- Interest Payments on Debt - 6%

When the U.S. Constitution was written, the authors knew the American economy would be affected by the Constitution. As you saw on the previous page, Congress has powers of taxation, spending, and borrowing. Congress has even more economic powers, such as printing money, regulating commerce, regulating foreign trade, and regulating banking.

There are some economic terms every student of the Constitution should know:

1. Gross Domestic Product (GDP). This is one of the most common indicators used to track the health of a nation's economy. It is measured in dollars. It is the total value of all goods and services produced in our country in one year. *Goods* are all the items we make (cars, furniture, clothing, televisions, etc.). *Services* are considered the value of using the labor and knowledge of people (like services of your dentist, local police, auto repair shop, etc.). Today the gross domestic product of the United States is more than $24 trillion.

2. National Debt. The *national debt* is the total amount of money the federal government owes. Currently, the national debt of the United States exceeds $30 trillion. In 2020 alone, Congress approved $2.4 trillion to combat the coronavirus and the resulting support to the American people and businesses.

This debt accumulates each year the federal government spends more than it receives. If you look at the chart on the previous page, you will see that the federal government forecasts to receive $3.8 trillion in revenue and spend $4.8 trillion. This means it would pay almost $1 trillion more than it received in taxes. The result would be the national debt increasing by this $1 trillion shortfall.

3. The Deficit. As stated above, the federal government often spends more than it takes in (especially in recent years). The amount of that annual (yearly) debt is called the *deficit*. A *surplus* is the opposite of a deficit and means that the government receives more money than it spends for a particular year. In the fiscal years 1998 through 2001, the federal government recorded a surplus. Since then, we have been in a deficit situation.

You and the Debt

If you had a part-time job and earned $2,415 a year and spent $2,770, you would be in debt. Your deficit would be $355. To pay off this debt, you would have to borrow $355. This example relates directly to that of the federal government, with the exception being that they are dealing in billions of dollars. If you were to divide the national debt by the population of the United States, you would see that each person accounts for more than $91,000 of this debt.

Government Spending

Why does the government spend more money than it actually has? Well, there are many demands for government spending in a democracy. We have many needs in this country: national defense, public health, disaster relief, quality education, etc. These are just a few of the items a government needs to provide, and these services are costly. Raising taxes higher and higher to pay for these needs is not very popular with Congress and may actually harm the economy. In a democratic country like ours, the government must try to meet all these popular demands. Sometimes the government cannot cut these "necessary" expenditures, and our debt increases. One of the problems that result from a massive federal deficit is the high cost of borrowing the money to cover the debt. When the government borrows large amounts of money, it must pay interest on that money. If you look at the chart on the previous page, you will see that the interest on the debt accounts for $288 billion of the national budget. This is the fourth largest expenditure of the federal government.

The Economic Outlook

The economic outlook for 2022 and 2023 in the United States is good, though inflation will remain high and other uncertainties exist. The war in Ukraine forced Russian sanctions, increasing the cost of certain commodities such as oil. The world hopes that Covid will have less impact, thanks to vaccinations and awareness. Most of the supply chain problems have also been labor problems, and the shipping and production issues will be slowly resolved. Inflation will remain high this year as our past stimulus keeps increasing prices. The near-term outlook is solid because of this past stimulus, but the later years bring a significant risk of recessions. The *Federal Reserve* will continue to set U.S. monetary policies to promote maximum employment and stable prices in the U.S. economy.

QUESTIONS

FILL IN THE BLANKS / SHORT ANSWER

1. Write the following large number:
   a billion _____ a trillion _____

2. What do the initials GDP stand for and what does it mean? _____

3. Give the current dollar figure for:
   GDP_____
   federal deficit _____
   national debt _____

4. When the government borrows money, it must pay this. _____

5. Each person accounts for how much of the national debt?_____

6. What is a surplus? _____

7. What is a recession? _____

8. What increases when the federal government has a deficit?_____

The following outline is for quick review and general reference purposes.

The Three Branches of American Constitutional Government

I. LEGISLATIVE BRANCH

A. Main Duty — make laws

B. Main Body is called Congress
1. Life of Congress begins on January 3rd every odd-numbered year, limited to two years
2. Sessions last from January to late in the year
3. Meets in Capitol Building, Washington, D.C.
4. Powers – See Article 1, Section 8
   Powers denied – See Article 1, Section 9
5. Lawmaking process
   a. Bills must be passed by both houses and sent to the president for approval
   b. Bill is law if signed; if not, Congress may attempt to pass by two-thirds vote in each house

C. Two Houses
1. House of Representatives
   a. 435 members divided among the states according to population of each state
   b. My city or town is in the ___ *Congressional District*
   c. _____is my representative
   d. Elected every two years on even-numbered years for two-year terms (take office in January of next year, an odd-numbered year)
   e. Qualifications: 25 years old, a citizen for seven years, an inhabitant of the state
   f. Special powers
      (1) initiate all revenue bills
      (2) start impeachment proceedings
      (3) select president if no candidate has Electoral College majority
   g. Officers
      (1) Speaker of the House, presently
      (2) Speaker elected from the House by majority party
      (3) Minority leader, Majority leader
   h. Salary
      (1) House $174,000
      (2) Speaker receives $223,500, plus expense allowances
   i. Representation
      (1) each state gets at least one member; membership based on population
      (2) sessions begin on January 3 and last until late in the year

2. Senate
   a. Two senators from each state, 100 senators
   b. One-third of senators elected every two years for six-year terms
   c. Qualifications: 30 years old, a citizen for nine years, an inhabitant of the state
   d. Senators from my state:

   _____   _____

   e. Special powers
      (1) approve nominations of president
      (2) approve treaties made by the president
      (3) try impeachments
   f. Salaries: $174,000
   g. Officers
      (1) President of the Senate is Vice President of the United States
      (2) Senate selects president pro tempore to act in the absence of the vice president
      (3) majority and minority leaders

D. Lawmaking Process
1. Bill is Introduced by Congress
2. Send to appropriate committee
   a. Hearings may be held
   b. Committee acts on bill; if favorably it will most likely come to floor vote, if unfavorably, it will most likely be killed.
3. Congress debates and votes
   a. If favorably acted on in committee and then passed on by the full house, it will be sent to the second house of Congress
   b. The next house takes similar action to that of the originating house
   c. If the bill passes without change, it is sent to the president
   d. If the bill does not pass, the bill is dead
   e. If they pass in different form, both houses must meet, represented by committees, to work out the differences. The new bill is then returned to both houses and voted upon again.
4. Presidential Action
   a. Before any bill can become law, it must be approved by the president.
   b. If the president vetoes a bill, Congress has the opportunity to pass the bill by two-thirds vote in each house. If it does, then the bill becomes law without the president's approval.
   c. If president decides to do nothing (and Congress is in session), after 10 days the bill will become law

continued

II. EXECUTIVE BRANCH

A. Main Duty — enforce laws

B. The President of the United States is chief officer
1. Qualifications: Natural-born citizen, 35 years old, resident of the United States for 14 years
2. Duties: foreign affairs, domestic administration, armed forces, national budget, legislation suggestions, acts on bills (approve or veto), appoints many officials, judicial functions; for complete description of powers, see Article 2

C. The Vice President
1. Duties
   a. President of the Senate
   b. First in order of presidential succession
   c. Assigned duties by the president
2. Qualifications are same as president

D. Salaries
1. President: $400,000, plus $150,000 expenses
2. Vice president: $230,700, plus expense allowance
3. Cabinet member: $199,700 salary each

E. Cabinet, 15 members
1. Secretary of State
2. Secretary of Defense
3. Secretary of the Treasury
4. Secretary of Agriculture
5. Secretary of Labor
6. Secretary of Commerce
7. Secretary of Interior
8. Secretary of Health and Human Services
9. Attorney General
10. Secretary of Housing & Urban Development
11. Secretary of Transportation
12. Secretary of Energy
13. Secretary of Education
14. Secretary of Veterans Affairs
15. Secretary of Homeland Security

III. JUDICIAL BRANCH

A. Main Duty — interpret laws, administer justice

B. Court System
1. Supreme Court
   a. Nine judges
      (1) selected by president, approved by Senate
      (2) serve for life, no special requirements
      (3) $213,900 salary; and chief justice salary is $223,500
   b. Duties
      (1) decide if laws brought before it are constitutional
      (2) hear cases of appeal on important matters
2. United States Court of Appeals
   a. There are 13 courts
      (1) each with three to nine judges, appointed by the president with Senate approval, for life terms
      (2) salary about 85 percent of Supreme Court justices
   b. Duties: hear cases of appeal from lower courts
3. United States District Courts
   a. There are 94 district courts
      (1) each court has one to 24 judges, appointed by the president; with Senate approval, for life terms
      (2) salary about 80 percent of Supreme Court justices
   b. Duties
      (1) ordinary trial courts
      (2) first court of contact on the federal level

C. The Constitution and the Courts
1. Courts are established by Article III of the Constitution
2. "The judicial Power of the United States, shall be vested in one supreme Court, and in such inferior Courts as the Congress may from time to time ordain and establish."
3. The power of the courts is extended to all cases arising under the Constitution, laws, and treaties of our nation.

D. Judicial Review
1. The courts interpret the Constitution, give it new and changing interpretations to meet modern conditions
2. Marbury v. Madison - precedent for judicial review
3. An essential addition to the system of checks and balances

Amending the Constitution

I. Two Ways of Proposing an Amendment
A. Congress proposes an amendment by two-thirds vote, which is the most common way.
B. Legislatures of two-thirds of the states require Congress to summon a Constitutional Convention to consider amendments.

II. Two Ways of Ratifying (approving) the Amendment
A. Three-fourths of the state legislatures approve (most common), or
B. Three-fourths of special state conventions approve.

The numbers in parentheses gives the page number where the answer or additional information may be found.

Development of the Constitution

1. Who wrote the Declaration of Independence? (5) _____
2. When and where was the Declaration signed? (5) _____
_____
3. What were the Articles of Confederation? (6) _____
_____
_____
4. Briefly describe some of the problems our country experienced under the Articles. (6)_____
_____
_____
5. When and where did the Constitutional Convention meet? (7-8) _____
_____
6. What major problem had to be solved during the Constitutional Convention between the large states and the small states, and what was the solution? (8) _____
_____
7. How did Thomas Jefferson feel about the new Constitution? (10) _____
_____
8. What was the purpose of the Preamble to the Constitution? (13) _____
_____
9. How many articles does the Constitution have? (14) _____
10. Which article gives information about the president? (14, 16, 30) _____
11. Which article tells you how to amend the Constitution? (14, 43) _____
12. How many amendments have been made to the Constitution? (14-15) _____

Legislative Branch

13. Explain what is meant by "representative" government. (12, 17, 23)_____
_____
14. Why are there staggered terms of office in the Senate? (18) _____
_____
15. What happens if a senator cannot finish a term? (18) _____
16. Who is president of the Senate? (18) _____
How many senators are there? (18) _____
17. How many senators does each state have? (18) _____ How long is the term? (18) _____
18. How many times may a senator be re-elected? (18) _____
19. What are the qualifications:
For a senator? (18) _____
For a representative? (19) _____
20. Explain the lawmaking process. (21-22) _____
_____
_____
21. Explain how sessions of Congress are numbered. (19)_____
_____
22. List the powers given to Congress by the Constitution. (17, 25) _____
_____
23. List the powers denied to Congress. (25) _____
_____
24. What is the "full faith and credit" clause? (28)_____

continued

25. What is the responsibility of the executive branch? (29-30) _____
_____

26. Who are the two most prominent officials in the executive branch? (29) _____
_____

27. What are the qualifications to be president and vice president? (29) _____
_____

28. How long is the president's term? (29) _____ How many terms may he/she serve? _____

29. Explain a "pocket veto." (21) _____
_____

30. What military powers does the president have? (30) _____
_____

31. On a separate piece of paper list the Cabinet positions and briefly explain their duties. (31-32)

32. Which house of Congress must approve presidential appointments? (18, 30)_____

33. Which house of Congress must approve treaties? (18) _____

34. Who may call a special session of Congress? (17, 30) _____

35. What happens if a president is unable to serve because of illness? (15, 29) _____
_____

36. What is the Electoral College? (33) _____
_____

37. On what date does the president take office? (29) _____

38. What are the five areas of presidential duties? (30) _____
_____

Judicial Branch

39. Name the three highest federal courts. (37)_____
_____

40. How many Supreme Court judges are there? (37) _____

41. How are federal judges selected? (15, 37) _____

42. How long do federal judges serve? (37) _____

43. Explain what judicial review is and how it affects the Constitution. (39-40) _____
_____

44. Which court would rule on the constitutionality of state and federal laws? (37) _____

45. What is the title of the chief official of the Supreme Court? (37) _____

46. Describe the two ways an amendment to the Constitution can be proposed. (43)_____
_____

47. Describe the two ways an amendment may be ratified. (43) _____
_____

48. List the important checks and balances that have been built into our government. (41-42) _____
_____

Vocabulary

Define the following terms.

49. ratify _____

50. amend _____

51. lobby _____

52. treaty _____

53. veto _____

54. federalism _____

55. compromise _____

The following test will help you prepare for your final Constitution test. It has questions similar to ones you will find on your final. It is suggested you write your answers on a piece of paper so you can take the test multiple times. You will find the correct answers at the bottom of **Page 53**.

MULTIPLE CHOICE

Write the letter of the correct answer in the space provided.

1. _____ The president may serve how many terms?   a. 1   b. 2   c. 3   d. 4

2. _____ What is NOT a rule of the flag code?
   a. worn flags should be thrown in trash   c. should be displayed on national holidays
   b. should be in the front of a parade   d. exact likeness should not be used in ads

3. _____ How many amendments have been added to the Constitution? a. 10   b. 21   c. 27   d. 41

4. _____ How many years is the president's term of office?   a. 2   b. 4   c. 6   d. 9

5. _____ What is the age requirement to become president?   a. 18   b. 21   c. 35   d. 45

6. _____ After a bill has gone through both houses of Congress successfully, it is sent to:
   a. the President   c. the Speaker of the House
   b. the States   d. the Supreme Court

7. _____ Which amendment gave women who are citizens the right to vote in all elections?
   a. 17th   b. 19th   c. 22nd   d. 27th

8. _____ How many U.S. senators come from each state?   a. 1   b. 2   c. 3   d. 4

9. _____ Each state receives at least _____ representative(s) in the U.S. House of Representatives.
   a. 1   b. 2   c. 3   d. 4

10. _____ Who may veto a bill proposed by Congress?
    a. the President of the United States   c. the Vice President
    b. the Secretary of State   d. all Cabinet members

11. _____ The president of the Senate is:
    a. the President of the United States   c. the Secretary of State
    b. the Speaker of the House   d. the Vice President

12. _____ Which of these rights is NOT an unalienable right from the Declaration of Independence?
    a. liberty   b. education   c. pursuit of happiness   d. life

13. _____ The Declaration of Independence was written largely by:
    a. Hamilton   b. Washington   c. Jefferson   d. Adams

14. _____ The national budget is presented annually to Congress by the:
    a. the Vice President   c. the Secretary of State
    b. the Governors   d. the President

15. _____ There are how many branches of government?   a. 1   b. 2   c. 3   d. 4

16. _____ The president takes the oath of office on:
    a. January 4th   b. January 20th   c. November 7th   d. September 5th

17. _____ In our First Amendment, which is NOT a "freedom"?
    a. freedom of the press   c. freedom of speech
    b. freedom of employment   d. freedom of religion

18. _____ The vote of what group really decides who will be president?
    a. Electoral College   c. United Nations
    b. popular vote by the people   d. House of Representatives

19. _____ What is described in Article 1, Section 8, of the Constitution giving Congress broad powers to write laws about new situations?
    a. war power   b. insight clause   c. elastic clause   d. inventional clause

20. _____ Which body has the power to borrow money?
    a. Congress   c. Executive Branch
    b. Supreme Court   d. State Legislatures

continued

MATCHING - Three Branches of Government

Write the letter of the correct answer in the space provided.

_____ 21. Has two houses

_____ 22. Is the court system of our country

_____ 23. Makes the laws

_____ 24. Enforces the laws

_____ 25. Described in Article 1 of the Constitution

_____ 26. Described in Article 3 of the Constitution

a. Executive Branch

b. Legislative Branch

c. Judicial Branch

MATCHING - The United States Congress

Write the letter of the correct answer in the space provided.

_____ 27. Has a six-year term

_____ 28. Meet in the Capitol Building

_____ 29. Elected every two years

_____ 30. Has the vice president as presiding officer

_____ 31. Has 435 members

_____ 32. Approves or rejects treaties

_____ 33. Passes bills they hope will become laws

_____ 34. Has 100 members

a. Senate

b. House of Representatives

c. Both the Senate and House

d. Neither the Senate nor the House

MATCHING - Cabinet Responsibilities

Write the letter of the correct answer in the space provided.

_____ 35. Chief legal officer

_____ 36. Manages Social Security

_____ 37. Carries out a war plan

_____ 38. Settles a strike

_____ 39. Foreign affairs

_____ 40. Secret Service

a. Secretary of State

b. Secretary of Defense

c. Secretary of Health & Human Services

d. Attorney General

e. Secretary of Labor

f. Secretary of Homeland Security

TRUE OR FALSE

*Write a **T** or **F** in the space provided.*

_____ 41. The Virginia Plan proposed two houses of Congress based on population.

_____ 42. The simple definition of democracy is government by the people, directly or through representation.

_____ 43. Senators are elected by the vote of the people in their state.

_____ 44. One-third of the Senate is elected every two years.

_____ 45. The largest U.S. state is Texas (in terms of population) receiving the most electoral votes.

_____ 46. The Constitution allows for laws to be made on subjects that did not even exist in 1787.

_____ 47. The original 13 colonies included Kentucky.

_____ 48. Your state legislature has the same lawmaking scope as the U.S. Congress.

_____ 49. Patrick Henry said, *"Give me liberty or give me death."*

_____ 50. Habeas corpus gives a prisoner the right to a fair trial.

_____ 51. Ben Franklin was president of the Constitutional Convention in 1787.

_____ 52. The building in which the Constitutional Convention met is called Independence Hall.

_____ 53. The Declaration of Independence was the nation's first Constitution.

continued

_____ 54. Our original Constitution outlawed slavery.

_____ 55. The Bill of Rights are the first 10 amendments to the U.S. Constitution.

_____ 56. The British held the Boston Tea Party to make friends with the colonists.

_____ 57. A U.S. senator may be re-elected only once, serving a maximum of two terms.

_____ 58. The House of Representatives has nothing to do with the impeachment of a president.

_____ 59. Under certain conditions, the House of Representatives selects the president.

_____ 60. A three-fourths vote is required for Congress to pass a bill over the president's veto.

_____ 61. After 10 days, a bill passed by Congress automatically becomes a law if the president doesn't act and Congress is still in session.

_____ 62. Supervising the coining and printing of money is the job of the Treasury Department.

_____ 63. An ex post facto law is a law that makes something illegal after the act has been committed.

_____ 64. Only federal officers may have titles of nobility.

_____ 65. Congress may not tax goods being exported from a state, even if the goods are going to a foreign country.

_____ 66. States must treat the citizens of other states the same way it treats its own citizens.

_____ 67. States can make treaties with foreign countries.

_____ 68. Both federal and state governments can establish courts.

_____ 69. The president can call both houses of Congress into special session

_____ 70. The Articles of Confederation was really our first constitution.

_____ 71. Federalism is the sharing of power by the federal government and state governments.

_____ 72. There are 12 Cabinet positions.

_____ 73. The U.S. Supreme Court justices are appointed by Congress.

_____ 74. The judicial branch has no checks on the other branches.

_____ 75. The U.S. flag should be in the rear of a parade or procession.

_____ 76. The 26th Amendment allows 18-year-olds to vote in federal and state elections.

_____ 77. There are 15 justices on the Supreme Court.

_____ 78. The Declaration of Independence came before the signing of the Constitution.

_____ 79. United States senators receive a higher salary than U.S. representatives.

_____ 80. Cabinet members are elected rather than appointed.

This is the end of your Federal Unit self-test. Please take the following steps:

1. Correct your test by using the answers below.

2. Any mistakes you have made should be reviewed, corrected, and studied.

3. You should take the test over, paying particular attention to any previous incorrect answers.

Your number of correct answers: _____

Your number of incorrect answers: _____

Total = **80**

Answers: 1. b 2. a 3. c 4. b 5. c 6. a 7. b 8. b 9. a 10. a 11. d 12. b 13. c 14. d 15. b 16. b 17. b 18. a 19. c 20. a 21. b 22. c 23. b 24. a 25. b 26. c 27. a 28. c 29. b 30. a 31. b 32. a 33. c 34. a 35. d 36. c 37. b 38. e 39. a 40. f 41. T 42. T 43. T 44. T 45. F 46. T 47. F 48. F 49. T 50. T 51. F 52. T 53. F 54. F 55. T 56. F 57. F 58. F 59. T 60. F 61. T 62. T 63. T 64. F 65. T 66. T 67. F 68. T 69. T 70. T 71. T 72. F 73. F 74. F 75. F 76. T 77. F 78. T 79. T 80. F

Indiana's history is rich and distinguished. The name Indiana simply means "lands of Indians." In its early history, many Native Americans lived in this region.

There were at least 12 different Native American tribes in Indiana when the first Europeans arrived in the late 1600s. These groups included the Miami, Piankashaw, Wea, Shawnee, and Mahican. As the white settlers moved westward, many of the Native Americans were forced out of the region now known as Indiana. By 1838 few Native Americans remained in the state.

In 1679, Frenchman Robert Cavalier La Salle became the first European to cross the region. La Salle and others were searching for a water route to the Pacific Ocean, along with expanding the fur-trading industry.

Later in the 1600s, more Frenchmen followed, exploring, mapping, and building missions, forts, and trading posts. *Vincennes* became the first permanent settlement in Indiana about 1732 and later became the first territorial capital.

The rivalry between Great Britain and France in North America led to a series of wars. One of the last battles, *The French Indian War (1754-1763)* ended with the British gaining control of all land east of the Mississippi River, including Indiana. The new American residents in the 13 colonies were most interested in the westward movement and this land.

British troops did not enter the Indiana region until 1777 when fighting during the *Revolutionary War (1775-1783)* erupted here. George Rogers Clark of Virginia led American soldiers into Indiana to fight Britain and claim Indiana as American land. Their victory of 1770 at Fort Sackville in Vincennes, let to American control of the Northwest. After the Revolutionary War ended in 1783, the United States gained control of all land east of the Mississippi River. A plan had to be devised to settle state claims to the new land, and the *Northwest Ordinance of 1787* was passed. This federal law provided that this Northwest Territory would be the land divided into not less than three, nor more than five, states. In addition, a governor and council were appointed to pass laws. One of the most important provisions of this ordinance was the establishment of townships, providing land for public schools. This promoted free public education in the new territory.

In 1800, Congress created the *Indiana Territory* out of the western part of the Northwest Territory. This vast territory had only about 5,500 settlers and included what is now Indiana, as well as Michigan, Wisconsin, Illinois, and parts of Minnesota. William Henry Harrison became the first governor of the Indiana Territory and then later the ninth president.

William Henry Harrison

The size of the Indiana Territory was reduced over time with Michigan and Illinois splitting off. In November of 1816, the first General Assembly of 29 representatives, ten senators, and the lieutenant governor met in the capitol building in Corydon. On December 11, 1816, Indiana was admitted to the Union as the 19th state. People from other parts of the United States and Europe saw Indiana as a place where new opportunities exist.

In its first 50 years, Indiana saw farming replace fur-trading as the chief occupation of the region. The economy improved in the 1850s, as railroad expansion linked Indiana to East Coast markets. Manufacturing involved farm machinery, tools, and pork processing that were created to support the growing American economy. Because of its soil and climate, along with its central location, Indiana continues to be a base for agricultural and manufacturing industries.

The state capital moved from Corydon to Indianapolis in 1825 and remains today. The central location was important for managing and growing the state. As Native Americans moved west, there were vast amounts of land open for settlement. The young state's settler population rose sharply from 147,000 in 1820 to more than a million in the 1850s.

continued

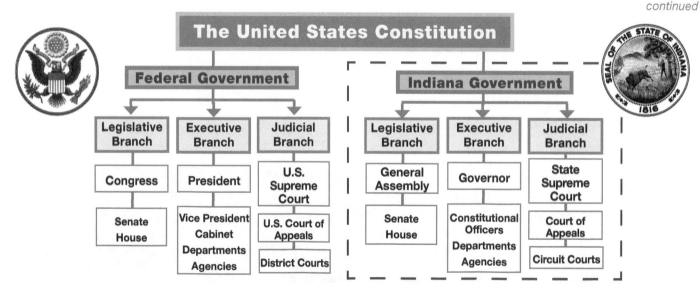

The U.S. Constitution splits governing powers between the federal government and the states. This unit will cover the state government portion of the chart above. It will also include the study of local government bodies.

In April 1861, the southern states, angry over President Abraham Lincoln's administration and views, created the Confederate forces that went to war against Union forces. This was the beginning of the *American Civil War (1861-1865)*. Indiana mainly supported the Union war effort and contributed nearly 200,000 troops. The postwar era in Indiana included substantial growth as mining and natural gas exploration aided the economy.

With the building of large oil refineries and steel mills, Indiana began creating more jobs. One of the first gasoline-powered cars was developed by Elwood Haynes of Kokomo in 1894. This created an influx of manufacturing plants that rivaled Detroit. In 1909, The Indianapolis Motor Speedway opened as a testing and racing facility.

Indiana changed and modified its government as its population and economy have evolved. The development of a state constitution started with the Northwest Ordinance of 1787. This ordinance set criteria that individual territories had to meet to qualify for statehood, the main one being that the population of the area had to reach 60,000 inhabitants. When the Indiana Territory met those criteria, the United States Congress passed an enabling act (April 16, 1816), authorizing it to adopt a state constitution and form a state government. In May that same year, the constitutional convention delegates worked quickly to create a new state constitution.

Indiana Constitutions

s

The state of Indiana has had only two constitutions. The first, as mentioned above, was written in 1816 when Indiana sought entry into the Union. This outlined the basic structure and functions of the new government. Only white male citizens over the age of 21 who had lived in Indiana for one year could vote. Slavery in Indiana was prohibited. However, this law did not apply to slaveholders who lived in Indiana before the constitution took effect.

By 1851, Indiana was struggling with debt and being poorly managed with the citizens voting to amend the original constitution. Improvements were made in several areas: (1) provided for term limits, and the elections of government officials, (2) fiscal controls and taxation process, (3) prohibited special laws that benefited only certain individuals or classes of people. The *Constitution of 1851* continues to be the constitution of the state, although there have been numerous amendments passed over the years.

Organization of State Government

You have seen in studying the U.S. Constitution that certain responsibilities are left to the states. To carry out these responsibilities, states have set up state constitutions. The state government, for example, is responsible for state highway construction, local laws, intrastate commerce, traffic laws, education, marriage and divorce laws, hospitals, voting regulations, and so on. The federal government has certain other responsibilities; for example, national defense, foreign affairs, coinage of money, and so on.

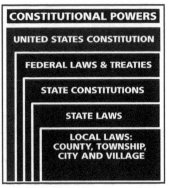

CONSTITUTIONAL POWERS
UNITED STATES CONSTITUTION
FEDERAL LAWS & TREATIES
STATE CONSTITUTIONS
STATE LAWS
LOCAL LAWS: COUNTY, TOWNSHIP, CITY AND VILLAGE

The chart shows where the state constitution fits regarding authority and power. While each of the 50 states has its own constitution, all provisions of state constitutions must comply with the United States Constitution. The 10th Amendment recognizes the powers of state governments.

The organization of state government is very similar to that of the federal government. Both have three branches, and these three branches have about the same types of duties in the state as they have in the federal government. The same type of checks-and-balances system applies to each and both have bills of rights. There are other similarities and some differences that you will notice as you read about the Indiana Constitution.

QUESTIONS

TRUE OR FALSE? Write a *T* or *F* in the space provided.

____ 1. The Indiana Territory was established in 1800.

____ 2. Indiana has had four constitutions.

____ 3. One of the first white man to explore Indiana was Robert Cavalier La Salle.

____ 4. Indiana became a state in 1861.

____ 5. Michigan was once part of the Indiana Territory.

____ 6. The capital of Indiana is Fort Wayne.

____ 7. The U.S. took control of the Indiana Territory from the French.

____ 8. Foreign affairs is the duty of state government.

____ 9. Both the Indiana Constitution and the U.S. Constitution have a bill of rights.

____ 10. States may make treaties.

MATCH THE PERSON. Write the letter from *Section B* in the space that matches the person in *Section A*.

A	B
1. William Henry Harrison ____	a. Developed one of the first gasoline powered cars
2. Elwood Haynes ____	b. First European to visit this region
3. R.C. La Salle ____	c. President during Civil War
4. George R. Clark ____	d. First Governor of Indiana Territory ____
5. Abraham Lincoln ____	e. Helped defeat British Rule

EVENTS IN ORDER. Write the numbers **1 - 4**, indicating which historical event happened *first (1)*, *second (2)*, *third (3)*, or *fourth (4)*.

_____ State capital moved to Indianapolis.

_____ Indiana becomes a state.

_____ United States Constitution signed.

_____ Current Indiana Constitution approved.

As we have learned, Indiana's journey to statehood dates back to the *Ordinance of 1787* and the creation of the *Northwest Territory*. As America began to expand westward, the Northwest Territory was an important governmental region established within the early United States. The area encompassed what is now Ohio, Indiana, Illinois, Michigan, Wisconsin, and part of Minnesota.

Westward Expansion

The *Treaty of Paris*, signed on September 3, 1783, between the American colonies and Great Britain, ended the American Revolution and formally recognized the United States as an independent nation. Two important provisions of the treaty were British recognition of U.S. independence and gaining all territory between the Allegheny Mountains on the east and the Mississippi River on the west. Now the challenge for our leaders in the United States was to develop the process for settlement and division of the Northwest Territory.

The *Northwest Ordinances*, also called the *Ordinances of 1784, 1785,* and *1787*, gave the United States this orderly and equitable procedure for settlement. The Northwest Ordinance of 1787 was the most important of the three acts. It was the basis for the government of the Northwest Territory and allowed for the creation of at least three, but not more than five, states.

The Northwest Ordinance of 1787 established a three-step process for statehood:

1. Settlers came to a territory, and a governor was appointed.
2. Once the population totaled 5,000 free adult males who owned at least 50 acres of land, they could establish their own government.
3. Once the population grew to 60,000, the territory could then apply to Congress for statehood with its government and constitution.

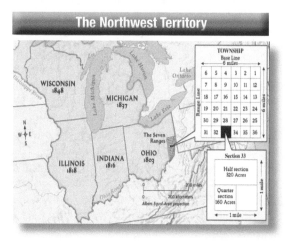

The Northwest Territory

These five states were the result of dividing up this region; the land was divided into townships six miles wide by 6 miles long, then divided again into 36 one-mile square sections that were intended for farms. You can still see this checkerboard pattern when you fly across the country on a clear day.

Indiana Becomes a State

Before Indiana became a state, it was known as the Indiana Territory. In March 1803, Ohio attained statehood, which left the rest of the former Northwest Territory as the Indiana Territory. Congress wanted the Indiana Territory surveyed in full in preparation for American colonization.

In late 1815, the Indiana Legislature sent a petition to the United States Congress asking to be admitted into the Union. The petition claimed that the Indiana Territory had met conditions required for statehood established by the Northwest Ordinance. Part of the process for being admitted as a state was for Indiana to adopt its own constitution. Delegates assembled at Corydon to write a constitution for state government in Indiana. The first constitution was modeled after the federal government and the state constitutions of Kentucky, Ohio, and Pennsylvania.

On December 11, 1816, President James Madison approved Indiana as the 19th state of the Union. The migration of people, industry, and culture to Indiana were the direct result of the Northwest Ordinance.

Principles of the Northwest Ordinance

The established ordinances were considered the most significant accomplishment of the Articles of Confederation; as it not only developed a process for admitting new states to the Union but also mandated that new states meet the following principles:

- *had to guarantee basic rights to the people, including religious freedom, the writ of habeas corpus, and trial by jury;*
- *outlawed slavery in this new land;*
- *encouraging education, allocating land for that purpose;*
- *exercised good faith when dealing with Native Americans.*

The states in the Northwest Territory would be equal to the original 13 states. They would have the same representation, which at the time gave each state two representatives in the Senate and one representative in the House for every 30,000 residents.

QUESTIONS

TRUE OR FALSE? Write a *T* or *F* in the space provided.

____ 1. Illinois was another state that was formed from the Northwest Ordinance.

____ 2. Michigan became a state before Indiana.

____ 3. The creation of a state constitution occured after being admitted to the Union.

____ 4. Slavery was outlawed in the new states formed from Northwest Territory.

____ 5. The original 13 colonies had more authority than the five newly established states.

EVENTS IN ORDER. Write the numbers *1 - 4*, indicating which historical events related to Indiana and the Northwest Ordinance happened *first, second, third,* or *fourth.*

_____ Northwest Ordinance is established.

_____ Indiana's first constitution is written.

_____ Treaty of Paris was signed.

_____ Articles of Confederation were ratified.

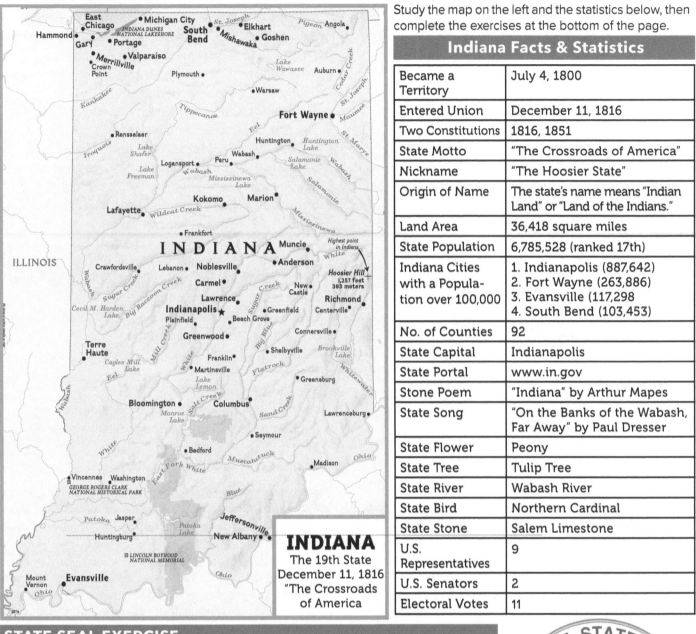

Study the map on the left and the statistics below, then complete the exercises at the bottom of the page.

Indiana Facts & Statistics

Became a Territory	July 4, 1800
Entered Union	December 11, 1816
Two Constitutions	1816, 1851
State Motto	"The Crossroads of America"
Nickname	"The Hoosier State"
Origin of Name	The state's name means "Indian Land" or "Land of the Indians."
Land Area	36,418 square miles
State Population	6,785,528 (ranked 17th)
Indiana Cities with a Population over 100,000	1. Indianapolis (887,642) 2. Fort Wayne (263,886) 3. Evansville (117,298 4. South Bend (103,453)
No. of Counties	92
State Capital	Indianapolis
State Portal	www.in.gov
Stone Poem	"Indiana" by Arthur Mapes
State Song	"On the Banks of the Wabash, Far Away" by Paul Dresser
State Flower	Peony
State Tree	Tulip Tree
State River	Wabash River
State Bird	Northern Cardinal
State Stone	Salem Limestone
U.S. Representatives	9
U.S. Senators	2
Electoral Votes	11

INDIANA
The 19th State
December 11, 1816
"The Crossroads of America"

STATE SEAL EXERCISE

To the right is a reproduction of the official *Great Seal of Indiana*. It was approved as the official state seal design by the 1963 General Assembly. *Research the "Great Seal" and answer the following questions:*

1. Do you think the sun is rising or setting, and what would that represent?

_____

2. What type of tree is the leaf from, shown on the outer edge?_____
3. What is the name of the hills in the background? _____
4. Why was a buffalo included on the seal? _____

GEOGRAPHY AND MAP EXERCISE

1. Circle the highest point in Indiana. What is the elevation? _____
2. On the map, identify the *Ohio River* (with an "**O**"), *Wabash River* (with a "**W**") and *Lake Michigan* (with a "**L**.")
3. Identify the four largest cities in Indiana by placing the numbers **1 - 4** on the cities location.
4. On the map, identify all the states that border Indiana. _____
5. On the map, identify the location of your hometown and indicate the spot with a star.
6. Name two Indiana cities that are on the shore of Lake Michigan. _____
7. What city hosts the state capital? _____

Indiana's current constitution dates back to 1851, which replaced an earlier constitution that had been utilized to obtain statehood. The fact that it was written sixty-four years after the U.S. Constitution is helpful because the language used in the document is more like present-day English and helps shed light on how the Hoosiers who authored our constitution interpreted the U.S. Constitution. The complete state constitution is available on the Indiana website at *www.IN.gov*.

The Indiana Constitution provides the fundamental law on matters relating to the organization and operation of the Indiana state government. It is subject only to the restrictions of the United States Constitution and acts of Congress. This constitution may be changed only by voter approval of proposed amendments.

A brief description of each article of the constitution is listed below:

Preamble

The preamble is similar to the preamble in the U.S. Constitution and explains why the Indiana Constitution was written. Below is the wording:

"TO THE END, that justice be established, public order maintained, and liberty perpetuated; WE, the People of the State of Indiana, grateful to ALMIGHTY GOD for the free exercise of the right to choose our own form of government, do ordain this Constitution."

Article 1 - Bill of Rights

There are 37 sections of the Indiana Bill of Rights. Many of these sections were based on provisions in the U.S. Constitution. The 14th Amendment to the U.S. Constitution prohibits states from depriving any person of life, liberty, or property without the due process of law. Some of the Indiana Bill of Rights goes beyond the rights established by our U.S. Constitution.

The topics to the Indiana Bill of Rights in Article I are listed below:

Section 1	Natural rights
Section 2	Right to worship
Section 3	Freedom of thought
Section 4	Freedom of religion
Section 5	No religious test for office
Section 6	No state money for religious institutions
Section 7	Competency of witness
Section 8	Oath, how administered
Section 9	Free speech and writing
Section 10	The truth in libel
Section 11	Unreasonable search and seizure
Section 12	Courts and the administration of justice
Section 13	Rights of accused, rights of victims
Section 14	Double jeopardy and self-incrimination
Section 15	Rights of persons arrested
Section 16	Excessive bail, punishment, penalties
Section 17	Bailable offenses
Section 18	Penal code and reformation
Section 19	Jury in criminal cases
Section 20	Civil cases, right of trial by jury
Section 21	Compensation for services and property
Section 22	Debts, imprisonment exemption
Section 23	Equal privileges and immunities
Section 24	Ex post facto laws
Section 25	Taking effect of laws
Section 26	Suspension of laws
Section 27	Habeas corpus
Section 28	Treason defined
Section 29	Treason, proof
Section 30	Effect of conviction
Section 31	Right of assemblage and petition
Section 32	Right to bear arms
Section 33	Military
Section 34	Restrictions upon soldiers
Section 35	No titles of nobility
Section 36	Freedom of emigration
Section 37	Slavery prohibited

Article 2 - Suffrage and Elections

Article 2 sets up voting qualifications and election laws. The title of this section refers to "suffrage," which is an individual's right to vote in political elections. In addition to voter's rights, it also established the timing of elections. The desire is to have many state elections at the same time, thus increasing voter turnout (the general election is held the first Monday of November in even-numbered years).

Article 3 - Distribution of Powers

Article 3 of the Indiana Constitution divides the state government into three branches: the legislative, the executive, and the judicial. The fundamental principle of separation of powers has existed in state and local governments from the earliest times. Unlike the national government, which has only the powers that are outlined in the U.S. Constitution, state governments have all authorities not denied it by the United States or Indiana Constitution.

Article 4 - Legislative

Article 4 provides rules for the legislative branch of Indiana government, known as the General Assembly. Similar to the U.S. Congress, the General Assembly is divided into two houses, the Senate and the House of

continued

Representatives. The Legislature has direct authority over local government units, such as counties, townships, and special-purpose districts.

Article 5 - Executive

Article 5 outlines the powers and duties of the state-elected offices, including the governor and the lieutenant governor. The executive power shall be vested in a governor who is "to take care that the laws are faithfully executed."

Article 6 - Administrative

Article 6 mentions the executive and administration positions that are not under the governor's authority, including the elective-state offices created by the constitution. These offices include state officials such as a secretary of state, an auditor, and a treasurer. Also mentioned is the duties and requirements for county and township officers.

Article 7 - Judicial

Article 7 vests the power of the judiciary branch into three courts, the Indiana Supreme Court, the court of appeals, and the circuit courts. The Indiana court system is similar to the federal court system.

Article 8 - Education

Article 8 establishes the state's public school system under the direction of the State Superintendent of Public Instruction. Included is the crucial aspect of funding schools and quality education.

Article 9- State Institutions

Article 9 gives the duty to the general assembly to provide support and guidance for citizens of the state with special needs. In addition to people with vision or hearing ailments, it also assists with juvenile offenders and mental health treatments.

Article 10 - Finance

Article 10 establishes the state's revenue power, including how the state can collect money (revenue) from the people through taxes on property, income, and sales. It explains how public funds are budgeted, spent, and audited.

Article 11 - Corporations

Article 11 provides for general banking laws and the regulations surrounding banks, loans, and payments to creditors.

Article 12 - Militia

Article 12 establishes rules for the state militia and authorizes the governor as the commander-in-chief of the militia.

Article 13 - Municipal Debt

There is only one section of this article establish rules for debt limitations.

Article 14 - Boundaries

Article 14 describes the boundaries of the state and the jurisdiction with other states that share rivers.

Article 15 - Miscellaneous

Article 15 has a variety of subject matter that did not fit well into other sections. Some of these include the duration of public offices, the official oath of office, the state seal, and areas of counties.

Article 16 - Amendments

Article 16 explains how the Indiana Constitution can be changed and sets up the necessary procedures. An amendment to the state constitution may be proposed in either branch of the General Assembly. Once approved by a majority of its members, the governor must sign it, and then the proposed amendment is presented to the next General Assembly. If agreed to by the second General Assembly, the amendment must be placed on the state election ballot and ratified by a majority of the voters. For example, if an amendment is approved by the 121st General Assembly, it must also be passed by the 122nd General Assembly, before it is presented to the voters of the state.

The current constitution has been in effect since November 1, 1851, when it replaced an earlier constitution from 1816. The lengthy process to change the state constitution means Indiana has had very few amendments. Only 49 amendments to the 1851 Constitution were adopted. The Indiana Constitution is the eighth oldest in the country and the fourth shortest constitution, with 11.610 words.

State Constitution vs U.S. Constitution

Initially, state constitutions were short and brief. Today the 50 state constitutions average about 30,000 words. In comparison, the United States Constitution has 7,591 words (including the 27 amendments). Like the U.S. Constitution, state constitutions provide a framework of government that includes three branches. State constitutions are longer because they have many details and often address topics unique to the state. It is easy for these to become outdated; thus, state constitutions are more open to amendments. Remember that the U.S. Constitution leaves the details to the lawmakers in Congress and the courts. This makes the U.S. Constitution very flexible and state constitutions often inflexible.

As new states were created and state constitutions were needed, they would benchmark not only the U.S. Constitution but other existing states. The framers of Oregon's constitution copied extensively from the Indiana Constitution and borrowed liberally from

continued

other state constitutions. These men were mainly from the states around Indiana, so it is expected that its constitution would reflect their beliefs about the proper role of government.

Separation of Powers in Indiana

The system of checks and balances reinforces the separation of powers concept. Not only is power divided, but one branch checks the other branches. For example, the courts have the power to declare laws and executive actions unconstitutional. The governor can veto bills from the legislature. The legislature must approve the government's budget and many of the governor's appointments. These are all examples of the constitution's attempts and ultimately of the people to avoid concentrating too much power in one place. The people always retain the right to control government by amending the constitution and rewriting state constitutions.

QUESTIONS

WHICH ARTICLE? In which article of the state constitution would you find information on the following? (Give section number when possible.)

1. State elections _____
2. The governor _____
3. Jury trial _____
4. Religious freedom _____
5. Mental health institutions _____
6. The judicial system _____
7. Revising the state constitution _____
8. Voter qualifications _____
9. Separation of powers _____
10. Public school system _____

TRUE OR FALSE? Write a *T* or *F* in the space provided.

____ 1. Voters must approve changes in the state constitution.
____ 2. The Indiana Constitution has equal powers to the U.S. Constitution.
____ 3. An amendment to the state constitution may be proposed in either house of the Legislature.
____ 4. The Indiana Constitution helps establish federal laws and treaties.
____ 5. State constitutions are always shorter in length and contain fewer details than the U.S. Constitution.
____ 6. Freedom of speech is not listed in the Indiana Constitution, only in the U.S. Constitution.
____ 7. Right to bear arms is not listed in the Indiana Consitution, only in the U.S. Constitution.
____ 8. There are more amendments in the U.S. Constitution than in the Indiana Constitution.
____ 9. The 26th Amendment of the U.S. Constitution establishes the voting age in Article 2 of the Indiana Constitution.
____ 10. There are 12 executive branch officers listed in the Indiana Constitution.
____ 11. The three branches of government are used to keep powers balanced and in check.
____ 12. The state seal is shown on Indiana state flag.

FILL IN THE BOXES (CHECKS & BALANCES)

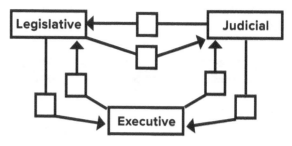

a. governor can grant pardons to those convicted
b. proposes laws to avoid judicial decision rulings
c. may pass laws by overriding a governor's veto
d. may declare laws from the General Assembly unconstitutional
e. may veto laws passed by the General Assembly
f. may declare executive orders unconstitutional

System of Checks and Balances in the State of Indiana

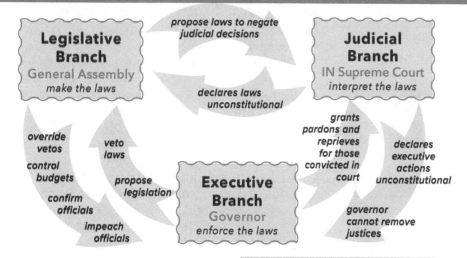

Legislative Branch
General Assembly
make the laws

propose laws to negate judicial decisions

declares laws unconstitutional

Judicial Branch
IN Supreme Court
interpret the laws

override vetos
control budgets
confirm officials
impeach officials

veto laws

propose legislation

Executive Branch
Governor
enforce the laws

grants pardons and reprieves for those convicted in court

declares executive actions unconstitutional

governor cannot remove justices

*All state governments are modeled after the federal government and have three branches: executive, legislative, and judicial. The principle guiding federal and state constitutions is the **separation of powers**. The distribution of power with a system of **checks and balances** does not allow any single branch of government to have too much power. Some of the most critical "checks" by the branch are listed in the shaded arrows.*

The Indiana Constitution
PRESENT ONE ADOPTED IN 1851

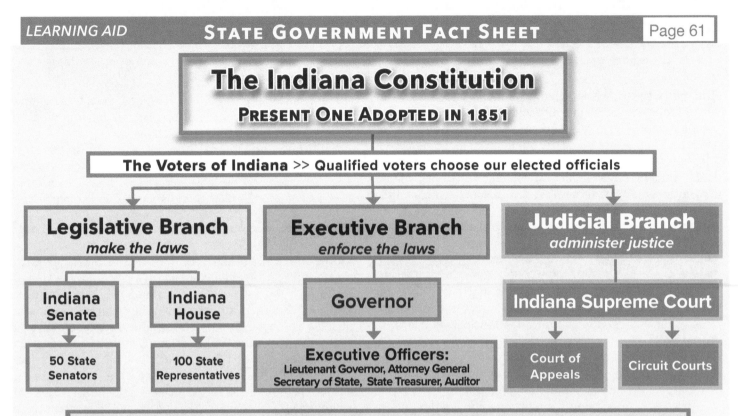

The Voters of Indiana >> Qualified voters choose our elected officials

Legislative Branch
make the laws

Executive Branch
enforce the laws

Judicial Branch
administer justice

Indiana Senate → 50 State Senators

Indiana House → 100 State Representatives

Governor → **Executive Officers:** Lieutenant Governor, Attorney General Secretary of State, State Treasurer, Auditor

Indiana Supreme Court → Court of Appeals / Circuit Courts

Legislative Branch Quick Facts
The Indiana General Assembly is made up of the state Senate and state House of Representatives.

body	members	terms	age reqt.	salary	qualifications
Senate	50	4 years	25	$28,103	Must be a citizen of the United States and a resident of their district for one year
House	100	2 years	21		

Executive Branch Quick Facts
The Consitution provides for executive officers.

officer	terms	salary	notes
Governor	4 years	$134,051	must be at least 30 years of age, must be a citizen of the United States for 2 years, and a qualified voter of Indiana, have lived in Indiana for at least 5 years
Lt. Governor	4 years	$103,076	same qualifications as governor; elected jointly with the governor
Attorney General	4 years	$107,686	represents the legal interests of Indiana
Secretary of State	4 years	$89,514	manages public documents and keeper of the Great Seal
State Treasurer	4 years	$89,514	responsible for the custody and spending of state money
Auditor	4 years	$89,514	ensures bills are paid and that state agencies are spending money wisely

*Other important executive officers are the clerk of the courts, superintendent of public instruction., and heads of various departments.

Judicial Branch Quick Facts
The Indiana Court System

Circuit Court	Court of Appeals	Supreme Court
• organized within 90 judicial circuits	• organized into five judicial districts	• final court of appeal for state matters
• chief trial court of the state, one located in each county	• three justices hear each appellate case, total of 15 judges in court of appeals	• five Supreme Court judges, commission selects a member to act as chief justice for a five-year term
• may hear appeals from city and town courts	• judges elected by the voters in each district to 10-year terms	• judges are selected by a nominating commision then re-elected by voters
• judges elected by the voters in each circuit to six-year terms	• a panel of three judges hears the appeals and makes a ruling	• all courts of the state are under the supervision of the IN Supreme Court

"The Legislative authority of the State shall be vested in a General Assembly, which shall consist of a Senate and a House of Representatives." — Indiana Constitution, Article 4

The purpose of the legislative branch is to make the laws. Indiana's legislative branch is called the *General Assembly* (or *legislature*) and consists of the Senate and House of Representatives. By sharing the same name as the federal Senate and House of Representatives, the state officers have similar duties and responsibilities. However, you must remember that the state legislature is responsible for lawmaking on a state-wide basis in Indiana, while the United States Congress in Washington, D.C. is responsible for national issues and laws.

General Assembly

The General Assembly is a part-time legislature with its members only in session for a few months each year. This group has a wide range of responsibilities. Here is a summary:

- makes (or enacts) Indiana laws
- levies taxes and determines where funds are spent to support the affairs of state government
- proposes amendments to the state constitution
- sets rules for the operation of Indiana's local governments
- has the power to impeach any state officer for crime or negligence
- oversees many activities of the executive branch

Legislative Sessions

Each Indiana General Assembly exists for two years and has one session annually, convening on the first Tuesday after the first Monday in January. During odd-numbered years, state law requires lawmakers to adjourn by April 29th; during even-numbered years, the legislature must conclude business by March 14th. Each chamber determines the number of working days during the session. Unfinished business may be carried over into the second year but may not be carried over into a new legislature.

The governor has the power to call for a *special session* to deal with immediate, essential issues. The special session must conclude within 40 days of being called by the governor. The multi-week session will allow legislators to review proposed bills through the entire legislative process, including committee hearings, public testimony, and floor votes. Recent special sessions have addressed inflation relief and abortion restrictions.

Each new legislature receives a new number. The legislature that began its term in 2021 was Indiana's 122nd General Assembly, the legislature that will start its term in 2023 will be the 123rd General Assembly, and so on.

Salary and Qualifications

Members of the General Assembly are elected by the people and can be re-elected. There are no term limits. Each senator and representative must be a citizen of the United States for two years, a resident of Indiana, and a resident of his or her district for one year. When elected, a senator must be at least 25 years of age and a representative at least 21 years of age. All legislature members receive an annual salary of $28,103, plus $183 for each day in session.

A *quorum* in each house is set at a majority of its members. Each house determines its own rules of procedure. No member can be expelled except by a two-thirds vote. Both houses may punish individuals for contempt or disorderly behavior.

Districts

In Indiana, all members of the legislature are elected from single-member districts. A district is determined by population rather than land area per the Indiana Constitution. Find out what district you live in and which officials represent you.

Every ten years, the federal government conducts a *census* to determine population changes. After these population changes are published, the districts are changed to correspond with census results. Changing a district's shape and size is known as *reapportionment*.

State Senate

There are 50 senate districts in the state of Indiana. Members are elected to four-year terms, with 25 of the 50 selected every two years. The state senate consists of one member from each district. Each member represents approximately 130,000 residents.

In addition to regular lawmaking powers, the Senate has special duties. One of these is to serve as the jury in cases of impeachment; another is to vote on appointments made by the governor.

Senate Leadership

The presiding officer of the state senate is the *lieutenant governor*, who may vote only to break a tie. He or she also ensures that the senate rules are being followed by its members. Another prominent official is the *president pro tempore* who presides over the Senate whenever the president of the senate is not available. Also, the pro tempore is responsible for setting the agenda of the senate.

The Indiana Statehouse is home to the General Assembly since 1888, the Capitol also houses the offices of the Governor, Lieutenant Governor, and the Supreme Court of Indiana. It is constructed of Indiana limestone and white oak.

continued

Both the majority party (currently Republicans) and minority party (currently Democrats) also elect a leader, assistant leaders, and a caucus chair. These leaders provide direction and advice to members on proposed legislation and party business.

State House of Representatives

There are 100 representative districts in the state. The House consists of one member from each district. Each district represents approximately 65,000 state citizens. All 100 members are elected to two-year terms in November of even-numbered years. Besides its duties of lawmaking, the house has the sole power to start impeachment proceedings. A majority of the members must vote in favor of commencing proceedings against an official.

House Leadership

The presiding officer of the House is known as the *speaker of the house* and is elected by the members themselves from the party holding the majority of seats. In the speaker's absence, the *speaker pro tempore* presides.

The majority party (currently Republicans) determines the nominee for speaker. The control of the House is with this majority party. Like the Senate president, the speaker has considerable power in deciding what legislation moves through the lawmaking process.

The speaker not only helps control the flow of legislation, but also the schedule for the House of Representatives, and when and if a bill is called for a vote. He or she also maintains order on the House floor, decides parliamentary issues, and works with minority leaders to resolve the problems that may be hindering legislation.

Both the House majority party and minority parties also elect a leader, deputy leaders, assistant leaders, and caucus chairpersons. These leaders provide direction and advice to members on proposed legislation and party business.

Contacting Your State Legislator

Each senator and representative has staff who specialize in helping you navigate state government. Sometimes it is difficult to know which federal, state, or local entity to contact for help. Your legislator's office can help point constituents (citizens of their district) in the right direction or help resolve specific issues with state government agencies.

Contact your state legislator for assistance with:

- Issues involving state agencies such as with education, jobs, and health programs.
- Expressing your opinion or concerns about pending legislation.
- Sharing an idea for new legislation.
- Requesting a commendation for outstanding accomplishments or milestones.
- Scheduling a visit or a tour of the Indiana Statehouse.
- Requesting a visit by or a meeting with your senator or representative.

QUESTIONS

WHICH BODY OF THE GENERAL ASSEMBLY?
The following details may closely match the state Senate or state House. In some cases, that may relate to both or neither of these. Answer **Senate (S)**, **House (H)**, **both (B)**, or **neither (N)**.

- ____ 1. Elected by the people.
- ____ 2. Have 100 members.
- ____ 3. Have 50 members.
- ____ 4. Are parts of the General Assembly.
- ____ 5. Receive salary of $28,103.
- ____ 6. The speaker is the presiding officer.
- ____ 7. The governor is the presiding officer.
- ____ 8. Term is always two years.
- ____ 9. Term is always six years.
- ____ 10. Start impeach proceedings.
- ____ 11. Must be at least 25 years old.
- ____ 12. Must live in district at least one year.
- ____ 13. Approves appointments of the governor.
- ____ 14. Declares laws unconstitutional.
- ____ 15. Considered the lower chamber.
- ____ 16. Republicans are the majority party.
- ____ 17. Tries impeachment cases.
- ____ 18. Meets in Indianapolis.
- ____ 19. Have term limits.
- ____ 20. Makes laws for every state.

VOCABULARY MATCH - Match the statement in *Section A* with the vocabulary word in *Section B*.

A

- ____ 1. A majority of members needed to conduct business in the Legislature.
- ____ 2. An award involving special praise.
- ____ 3. Willful disrespect or disobedience by a person in the Legislature.
- ____ 4. The process by which new legislative districts are drawn.
- ____ 5. The rules that govern the conduct of legislatures.
- ____ 6. A charge of misconduct against a government official.

B

a. impeachment   **b.** quorum   **c.** contempt
d. redistricting   **e.** parliamentary   **f.** commendation

NAME YOUR STATE LEGISLATORS

1. Who is your state senator? _____

   What number is your district? _____

2. Who is your state representative? _____

   What number is your district? _____

"Bills may originate in either House, but may be amended or rejected in the other; except that bills for raising revenue shall originate in the House of Representatives." —— Indiana Constitution, Article 4

Lawmaking in Indiana is, in many ways, similar to lawmaking at the federal level. The two houses of the Indiana General Assembly are patterned after the federal Congress, and have many of the same duties and responsibilities. Committees are used in the state lawmaking process similar to the federal government's lawmaking process.

Briefly speaking, a bill becomes law if it receives a majority of the votes cast in the General Assembly (26 of the 50 votes in the Senate, 51 of the 100 votes in the House) and gets the governor's approval. If the governor vetoes the bill, the General Assembly can override it by passing both houses with a majority vote. The lawmaking process is discussed in Article 4 of the Indiana Constitution and in more detail on the next page.

Special Rules for Bills

The Indiana Constitution mentions a few special rules about passing bills in the houses. Some of these are:

1. Bills are to be read on three different days (by title) before a final vote on passage.
2. Most bills are confined to one subject.
3. The governor has seven days to consider a bill passed by both houses, he or she may sign it or to return it with a veto. If the governor does nothing, the bill will automatically become law.

If a bill becomes law, it is sent to the secretary of state. A notice is printed in the newspaper advising the people of the new law. The bill is now known as an *act*. The declaration at the beginning of each new law is "Be it enacted by the General Assembly of the State of Indiana... ."

The death rate for bills is high. In each session of the legislature, more than 1,000 bills are introduced and voted on. While it varys, approximately 20 percent of the bills introduced become law. Bills can be reintroduced in subsequent sessions. Bills can, however, be reintroduced in subsequent sessions. Depending on the complexity of the legislation, it usually takes an average of three to five years to get a bill signed into law.

After a Bill Becomes Law

After passage, the enrolled act is printed, bound, and included in volumes that become *Acts of Indiana*. These new laws take effect July 1 of the year of passage unless otherwise specified in the enrolled act.

Notifying any individual or group affected by the law is also critical. For example, if the law creates a new service program, any individual affected by the law must know who is eligible for the program's services and how to access the services. The public must also be aware of any law requiring changes to everyday life.

Participating in the Legislative Process

In addition to our representatives proposing and approving laws, there are other opportunities for citizens to directly participate in our democracy. Every year the Legislature meets to engage in the process of public decision-making. The objective is to reach a consensus on a wide range of issues affecting every citizen and the future prosperity of Indiana. The process involves cooperation to make critical decisions in everyone's best interests.

We have chosen representatives to carry out the difficult task of determining which laws and policies will best serve these interests. However, legislators rely heavily on input from many different sources to perform their job effectively. They receive much technical information from their staff, state agency personnel, and professional lobbyists. However, much of what they decide depends on the views, interests, and preferences of the citizens who elect them.

This is precisely how the legislative process was designed to work. It is based on a close, open, positive relationship between elected officials and the citizens they represent. You can actively participate in the legislative process in a variety of ways. The following are a few ways to participate effectively:

- *Know How the Process Works* - Gather a basic understanding of the legislative picture and details of the lawmaking process. You are off to a good start with studying the materials in this book.
- *Make Yourself the Expert* - Do some homework before you address an issue. Thorough research allows you to present your viewpoint with confidence and credibility and, combined with your personal experience, is the most practical information you can provide.
- *Get to Know Your Legislators* - Develop a relationship with your legislators. Although you are unlikely to agree on every issue, you can still build a positive relationship in the long run. You can contact your legislators by making a personal visit, attending a Town Hall meeting, writing a letter, sending an e-mail message, or testifying before a committee.

Committees

Both houses of the General Assembly are organized into committees to help conduct business efficiently. There are standing committees that deal with ongoing subjects, such as education, public health, energy, agriculture, and labor. Some of these may meet in joint committees, made up of members of each house. The leader of each house may call a special committee to address a short-term bill. If a bill cannot be agreed on by both houses, it may be sent to a conference committee, where the differences may

continued

be resolved. And finally, an ad hoc task force may be appointed for a specific purpose. Legislators would be overwhelmed by the thousands of bills introduced each year if it were not for the committee system.

The process of making laws often seems inefficient, slow, and cumbersome. The process, however, has developed slowly over many generations. Much of what happens in the Legislature today is based on rules drafted by Thomas Jefferson for the Congress of the United States. Lawmaking is a slow process that promotes careful consideration and deliberation. This prevents hasty, thoughtless legislation and protects our rights as citizens.

Representatives and Restrictions

The selection of officers in the federal government often gets more publicity and voter participation than the election of state officers. This is unfortunate since many important state matters are close to our homes and jobs. These matters require talented and honest officials. The citizens of any state would do well to increase their interest in their state government.

While our legislators are making laws, they are free from arrest, except in exceptional cases, and cannot be prosecuted for their speeches in the General Assembly.

On the other hand, they have some restrictions:

1. They cannot receive an appointment by the governor to another public office.
2. Under Indiana law, some government officials may not legally serve in more than one public service position at any given time.
3. They, along with all other state officeholders, must file a statement of economic interests.
4. They cannot receive a salary increase during their term of office.
5. Neither house can adjourn without the consent of the other house. If they cannot agree on adjournment, the governor may adjourn the General Assembly.

In Indiana, there is no right of statewide *recall*, either of federal or state government officials, and no ability to recall members of the Indiana Legislature.

Lobbies in Indiana

Also found in Indianapolis during every session of the General Assembly are *lobbies*. These organized groups seek to influence lawmakers. Most of these lobbies operate legally under the laws controlling them, and some of them do a service of informing our lawmakers. However, there are instances where lobbies exert too much influence, and the views of other citizens are overlooked. There are more than 1,200 registered lobbyists in the state of Indiana. They represent business and industry, farmers, labor unions, teachers, veterans, women, professional and religious organizations, local governmental officials and many other groups.

Lawmaking Conclusion

The 50-member Senate and 100-member House together represent the over six million citizens of the state. The Indiana General Assembly allows for full citizen participation in the lawmaking process. Thousands of laws are the direct result of ideas generated by the people of Indiana.

It is a worthwhile experience to visit Indianapolis and observe your lawmakers at work. Although you cannot see the entire process in one visit, it can help you better understand lawmaking at the state level. Hopefully you will be able to see the action in a house session.

QUESTIONS

1. What are lobbies? Give an example. _____

_____

_____

TRUE OR FALSE? Write a *T* or *F* in the space provided.

___ 1. A two-thirds vote is required to pass a bill in the Senate or House.

___ 2. Bills may start in either house.

___ 3. The lawmaking process is discussed in Article 2 of the state constitution.

___ 4. Bills must cover at least three subjects.

___ 5. A bill must follow the same process in each house.

___ 6. The Legislature may overturn a governor's veto by a majority vote in the Senate and House.

___ 7. Legislators may hold only one additional public (government) job in the state.

___ 8. Most bills introduced are passed.

___ 9. Bills must be read on three different days before a final vote.

___ 10. If the governor does not act on a bill within seven days, it automatically becomes law.

VOCABULARY MATCH - Match the statement in *Section A* with the vocabulary word in *Section B*.

A

___ 1. A majority of members needed to conduct business in the Legislature.

___ 2. To stop a meeting with the intent to resume at a later time or date.

___ 3. Procedure for citizens removing government officials.

___ 4. Process by which new congressional districts are drawn.

___ 5. Laws to be considered.

___ 6. Another word for two branches of government.

B

a. adjourn   **b.** quorum   **c.** bicameral

d. legislation   **e.** redistricting   **f.** recall

1. Every state law starts with an idea.

The lawmaking process starts with an idea from you, the voting public, a state legislator, government agency, or someone may say to a legislator, "There ought to be a law for ...."

2. The bill is introduced.

A bill may start out in either the House or the Senate of the General Assembly. Each bill must be read by title three different days in each chamber before it can be passed.

3. Your state legislators at work, discussing and debating.

Indiana Senate - 50 Members

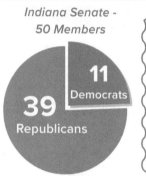

39 Republicans
11 Democrats

When the bill is first filed, it is assigned a bill number and read to the Legislature for the first time. Senators and representatives meet in small groups to research, discuss, and make changes to the bill. The state lawmaking process uses committees much like the federal government. Here the bill may have changes (amendments), get killed, get passed, have public hearings, or require more debate. Lobbyists may also meet with lawmakers..

Indiana House - 100 Members

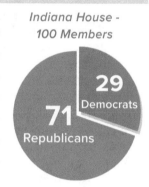

71 Republicans
29 Democrats

4. The Indiana General Assembly keeps favorable bills moving.

Approved by committee — If a majority vote favors the bill, it moves forward.

Second reading to the full legislative body — Amendments can still be proposed.

Third and final reading — After the final debate, the chamber votes on the bill. A simple majority is needed, 26 in the Senate and 51 in the House, for most bills to pass. Bills that are approved here move to the other chamber, following the same process.

Approval from the other chamber/house — Once both chambers agree on the same version of the final bill, it is sent to the governor.

5. Governor's action.

When the bill reaches the governor, he or she has seven days to take action. This may involve approving the bill by signing the bill into law, vetoing the bill, or doing nothing and the bill will automatically become law on the eighth day. Bills become effective on July 1 of the year they are enacted unless a different date is specified.

If a bill is vetoed, it can become law if both chambers of the General Assembly vote with majority to override the governor's veto. The bill then becomes a law without the governor's signature..

"The executive power of the State shall be vested in a Governor. He (or she) shall hold his office during four years, and shall not be eligible more than eight years in any period of twelve years." — Indiana Constitution, Article 5

The Governor

The executive branch of Indiana enforces and administers the laws. Besides enforcing and applying the law, the governor also has the critical duty of vetoing or approving bills passed by the Legislature. Elected by the people, the governor's role is to protect and serve the citizens. The governor is the most important officer in the executive branch.

Governor Eric Holcomb

The governor, as well as the lieutenant governor, must be at least 30 years old, a resident of the state for the five years preceding the election, a qualified voter of the state, and a U.S. citizen. Unlike the president, a governor does not need to be a natural-born citizen. The governor receives a salary of $134,051 and can be re-elected. The governor's term of office is four years. The governor is limited to two consecutive terms with at least four years before the same individual may hold the office again. Republican Governor Holcomb is term-limited and cannot seek re-election in 2024 to a third term in office.

The order of succession to the governor's office is; lieutenant governor; then the president pro tempore of the state senate. This succession noted in the state constitution was administered when Governor Frank O'Bannon died in office on September 13, 2003. Lieutenant Governor Joe Kernan was then sworn in as the new chief of the state.

Besides enforcing and administering the law, other essential responsibilities include:

1. The governor appoints many members of the state government. Many of these appointments require the approval of the state Senate. The governor may also remove any of these officials he or she feels are incompetent.

2. With the General Assembly's approval, the governor may reorganize any executive agencies in the state responsible to the governor.

3. The governor may grant pardons, commutations, and reprieves as he or she thinks proper.

4. The governor, at the beginning of each session and at the close of the governor's term of office, shall report to the General Assembly on the condition of the state.

5. The governor is the commander-in-chief of the state militia, except in cases of national emergency when they are called into federal service. (They are then under the control of the President of the United States.)

6. The governor may call special sessions of the General Assembly.

7. Each year, the governor must submit a state budget to the General Assembly for consideration.

8. The governor can appoint a replacement to a vacated seat in the U.S. Senate if that elected official leaves offices before a scheduled election.

In addition to the defined responsibilities above, a governor needs to be a strong leader. He or she must be savvy enough to navigate political divides and foster relationships among the members of the General Assembly.

In 2020, Governor Holcomb's leadership was put to the test dealing with the coronavirus and racial tensions throughout the state and country. Several *disaster proclamations* were issued to access federal funding and authorize executive actions to protect public health and safety. Serving as the state's chief spokesperson, the governor provides much-needed information and direction to state residents during these times.

Governor's Veto

As we have learned, both chambers of the General Assembly must agree on the same version of the bill before being sent to the governor, who may sign it into law or veto it. The governor's veto power allows the ability to take action on bills by a *regular veto* in which the whole bill is rejected, much like the president's veto.

Indiana is one of only six states that does not allow the *item* or *reduction* veto. Item veto is the ability to veto distinct lines or items within a bill while approving the remainder. This is common for *appropriation* bills where the governor simply changes the appropriation dollars.

The governor may decide to neither sign nor veto the bill, in which case it becomes law after seven days.

The Office of Governor

As we have learned, the governor's office is similar in some ways to the Office of the President of the United States. However, there are some differences. The most important differences are the lack of foreign affairs and national defense in the governor's responsibilities.

Indiana has had many famous and talented men serve as governor. (Indiana is one of 19 states that has never had a woman governor.) Thomas Riley Marshall was governor of the state from 1909 to 1913 and advocated labor and social legislation. He went on to become vice president to Woodrow Wilson in 1913. Indiana has yet to elect a woman governor. More recently, single-term governor Mike Pence was selected as President Donald Trump's vice president, serving from 2016 to 2020. The lives of these men make a worthwhile study.

Indiana Government Trifecta

A *trifecta* is when one political party holds the governorship, a majority in the state senate, and a majority in the state house in a state's government. Indiana has a Republican trifecta controlling the governor's office and both houses of the General Assembly. Republicans have had this trifecta for the past 14 years.

continued

Although the governor is probably the most well-known member of the executive branch, there are many other individuals who contribute to the smooth operation of state government. The Indiana Constitution provides for constitutional officers in addition to the governor; all have the same qualifications and term as the governor. The following are the executive officers and their duties:

Lieutenant Governor

Lt. Governor Suzanne Crouch

This officer is nominated at the party convention and is elected with the governor. The lieutenant governor receives a salary of $103,076 and include the following responsibilities:

- presiding over the state senate, ruling on parliamentary points and exercising tie-breaking votes;
- serving as governor if the current governor is unable to serve;
- chairing several different boards and councils, and serves on many committees, often acting as the governor's representative;
- serving as the director of the department of commerce and is the commissioner of agriculture.

Attorney General

This officer is the chief law enforcement officer of the state and the state's legal counsel. Some of the legal duties of this office are:

- providing legal and criminal investigation for the state, including investigating consumer complaints;
- providing legal representation for the state and advising state offices of their legal rights.

Secretary of State

The secretary of state and staff are primarily responsible for two areas: elections and business. The secretary of state:

- records, files, and certifies the public documents of the state, such as constitutional amendments, statutes, and election records;
- assist the Indiana Election Division to oversee candidate declarations and certifies election results;
- charters new businesses, protects investors in the securities industry, and issues trademarks;
- keeper of the state constitution and state seal.

State Treasurer

This elected official is the custodian of all state revenues and has the power to invest the state general fund and trust funds. This officer is responsible for agencies that handle property tax assessment and collection, income tax returns, investments of state money, and annual audits of local governments.

Auditor

This officer ensures the state's bills are paid with money held by the treasurer. This official examines the accounts of all state agencies to see if they are operating within the law, with respect to efficiency and economy, and reports the findings to the legislature and governor.

Clerk of the Courts

This officer receives and keeps records of cases in the state's three appellate courts" Supreme Court, Court of Appeals, and Tax Court.

Superintendent of Public Instruction

The superintendent of public instruction is chairman of the state board of education and directs the activities of the Indiana Department of Education.

Executive Department Organizations

Various departments of the executive branch are organized to carry out specific tasks of the branch. More than 70 state agencies, boards, and commissions that report to the governor and lieutenant governor. A great number of individuals are involved in the operation of the executive branch. Administering and enforcing state laws is a very difficult and challenging task. The individuals, who are members of this branch of state government, are important to the day-to-day operations of Indiana.

QUESTIONS

TRUE OR FALSE? Write a *T* or *F* in the space provided.

_____ 1. The General Assembly cannot be called into special session.

_____ 2. The governor may remove any officer he or she feels are incompetent.

_____ 3. The governor has the job of enforcing the law.

_____ 4. The governor's salary is $117,804.

_____ 5. The governor is in charge of foreign affairs.

_____ 6. The governor must be 35 years old or older.

_____ 7. State executive officers serve four-year terms.

_____ 8. The governor is elected at the same election as the president.

_____ 9. There is no limit on the number of terms a governor can serve.

_____ 10. The governor can only be impeached by the federal government.

WHICH STATE OFFICIAL? Which state official fits the statement given? Answer *Governor (G)*, *Lt. Governor (LT)*, *Attorney General (AG)*, *Secretary of State (SS)*, *State Treasurer (ST)*, or *Auditor (AD)*.

_____ 1. Appoints many department heads.

_____ 2. Is the commander-in-chief of the state militia.

_____ 3. Maintains the records of the General Assembly.

_____ 4. Is the chief law enforcement officer.

_____ 5. Invests state monies.

_____ 6. Represents the governor on boards and councils.

_____ 7. Would represent the state in court.

_____ 8. Examines the spending of state offices.

_____ 9. Submits the state budget to the General Assembly.

_____ 10. First in line to succeed the governor if needed.

_____ 11. Custodian of all state revenues.

_____ 12. Certifies election results.

"The judicial power of the State shall be vested in one Supreme Court, one Court of Appeals, Circuit Courts, and such other courts as the General Assembly may establish." —— Indiana Constitution, Article 7

The judicial branch of government in Indiana administers justice and interprets the laws. The state constitution provides that the judicial power of the state is vested in a supreme court, a court of appeals, circuit courts, and any other courts that the General Assembly chooses to establish. The judicial system is composed of a system of courts, each designed to fill a specific need.

Criminal and Civil Cases

All courts handle both *criminal* and *civil* cases. A criminal case involves a violation of a law for which there is a fine or other penalty like a prison sentence or probation. Criminal cases range from relatively minor offenses, such as traffic infractions, to serious ones, such as robbery or murder. These typical crimes are classified as *felonies*, *misdemeanors*, or *infractions*.

Felonies – Serious crimes that often are punishable by a state prison sentence or even death in the most extreme cases.

Misdemeanors – A lesser offense than a felony. It is punishable by fine or incarceration for less than a year in a city or county jail rather than in a state penitentiary.

Infractions – These are not punishable by jail or prison time but rather by a fine. The most common infractions are traffic violations.

Civil cases are brought against individuals or organizations by other individuals or organizations. In some civil cases, the plaintiff seeks money damages to be paid by the defendant. In other kinds of civil cases, the parties ask the court to take a certain action, such as to dissolve a marriage, decide the custody of minor children, review property rights, or stop someone from doing something.

Now that you are familiar with the type of court cases, it is time to learn more about the courts themselves.

Indiana Supreme Court

The final authority on the state constitution and the highest tribunal for any action started in the state courts, except when a federal question is raised, is the *Indiana Supreme Court*. The route to the Supreme Court usually begins in the lower courts, which have *original jurisdiction*. It will interpret disputed cases from the Indiana Court of Appeals and the Indiana Tax Court. The court reviews cases according to a calendar set by the chief justice. Other responsibilities include:

- admitting qualified persons to practice law in Indiana
- hearing appeals from defendants sentenced to death or for terms greater than 50 years
- insuring lower courts are hearing appropriate cases
- hearing cases (on petition) involving substantial questions of law, great public importance, or emergencies

Article 7 of the Indiana Constitution states that the Supreme Court must consist of between four and seven justices. Traditionally, the court consists of five justices appointed by the governor. A special judicial nominating commission recommends three potential

continued

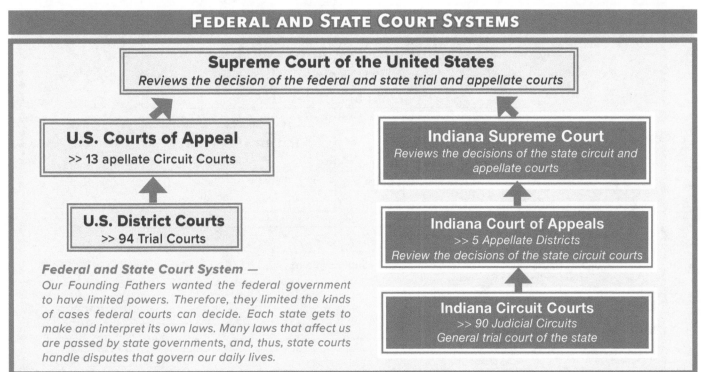

FEDERAL AND STATE COURT SYSTEMS

Supreme Court of the United States
Reviews the decision of the federal and state trial and appellate courts

U.S. Courts of Appeal
\>> 13 apellate Circuit Courts

U.S. District Courts
\>> 94 Trial Courts

Indiana Supreme Court
Reviews the decisions of the state circuit and appellate courts

Indiana Court of Appeals
\>> 5 Appellate Districts
Review the decisions of the state circuit courts

Indiana Circuit Courts
\>> 90 Judicial Circuits
General trial court of the state

Federal and State Court System —
Our Founding Fathers wanted the federal government to have limited powers. Therefore, they limited the kinds of cases federal courts can decide. Each state gets to make and interpret its own laws. Many laws that affect us are passed by state governments, and, thus, state courts handle disputes that govern our daily lives.

candidates when there is a vacancy. After an initial two-year appointment, the justice's name appears on a regular election ballot. Voters of the state will then decide if this justice should remain on the Supreme Court for the full 10-year term. There is no limit on the number of 10-year terms a justice may serve, but retirement is mandatory at age 75. The judicial nominating commission also selects one of the members to serve as chief justice of the court (for a term of five years). The courtroom and offices of the Supreme Court are located in the state capital.

Court of Appeals

The jurisdiction of the court of appeals is defined by the Indiana Constitution and the state Supreme Court. This court was created to relieve the growing caseload of the Supreme Court. Responsibilities include:

- receiving appeals from trial courts throughout Indiana (which are not slated for the Supreme Court)
- hearing appeals from criminal cases involving sentences of less than 50 years
- reviewing decisions involving administrative agencies such as the Worker's Compensation Board

Under a 1970 revision of the state constitution, the state is to be divided into geographic districts set by the General Assembly, and each district has three judges. This established five districts, with a total of 15 judges. The judges select one of their own to become chief judge, and each district elects a presiding judge. These judges are selected in the same manner and serve the same terms as the Supreme Court justices.

Tax Court

The *Indiana Tax Court* was established in 1986 to hear appeals involving the state's tax laws. These appeals come from decisions made by the Indiana Department of State Revenue, the Indiana Board of Tax Review, or other state agencies. Appeals from the tax court go directly to the Supreme Court. This special appellate level court has only one judge. The tax court judge is selected in the same manner (and serves the same 10-year term) as a Supreme Court or Court of Appeals judge.

Circuit Courts

Indiana is divided into 90 judicial circuits. A circuit refers to the geographic area served by the court. There is one court in each of 92 counties and two courts that jointly serve two counties. Ohio and Dearborn share one circuit, as do Jefferson and Switzerland counties. The circuit court is the chief trial court of the state. It has the power to try any case unless limited by local circumstances. The court may hear appeals from city and town courts. In areas without county-level courts, the circuit court establishes small courts to hear cases concerning minor offenses such as misdemeanors, ordinance violations, and civil suits involving less than $3,000. Except in Vanderburgh County, all circuit judges are elected every six years by the voters of each circuit.

Superior Courts

The General Assembly establishes the superior courts, and their organization and jurisdiction vary throughout the state.

continued

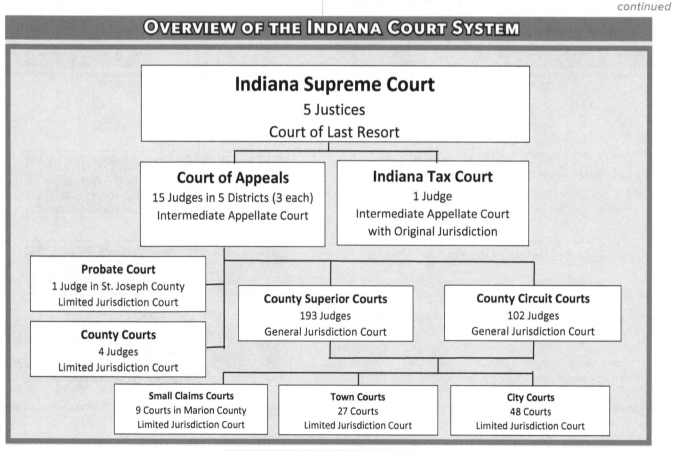

OVERVIEW OF THE INDIANA COURT SYSTEM

Indiana Supreme Court
5 Justices
Court of Last Resort

Court of Appeals
15 Judges in 5 Districts (3 each)
Intermediate Appellate Court

Indiana Tax Court
1 Judge
Intermediate Appellate Court
with Original Jurisdiction

Probate Court
1 Judge in St. Joseph County
Limited Jurisdiction Court

County Courts
4 Judges
Limited Jurisdiction Court

County Superior Courts
193 Judges
General Jurisdiction Court

County Circuit Courts
102 Judges
General Jurisdiction Court

Small Claims Courts
9 Courts in Marion County
Limited Jurisdiction Court

Town Courts
27 Courts
Limited Jurisdiction Court

City Courts
48 Courts
Limited Jurisdiction Court

They are courts of general jurisdiction and have the same powers as, and share cases with, the circuit courts. Some counties have separate superior courts, and some integrate them into a unified county court system. A superior court may have small claims and minor offenses divisions where there is no county court. In most counties, superior court judges are elected at a general election for a six-year term.

County Courts

In recent years there has been a move to restructure county courts into superior courts for more efficient processing of cases. There are now 31 county courts. They handle civil cases relating to contract, tort, or landlord/tenant issues where the damages do not exceed $10,000. Like circuit courts, county courts also handle misdemeanors and cases involving local ordinances, such as traffic violations. Appeals from the county courts go to the Indiana Court of Appeals. The county's voters elect the county judges to six-year terms.

Local Courts

Indiana communities are served by 48 city courts and 27 town courts. This group of courts' jurisdiction is minimal. Many are limited to handling misdemeanors, ordinance violations, and civil cases involving disputes less than $500. The more severe cases are heard in the circuit or superior courts. Judges in city and town courts are elected to four-year terms by their local voters. Some counties require that these judges be attorneys.

Habeus Corpus

The writ of habeas corpus, often shortened to habeas corpus, is the requirement that an arrested person be brought before a judge or court before being detained or imprisoned. Article 1, Section 27 of the Indiana Constitution states: "The privilege of the writ of habeas corpus shall not be suspended, except in case of rebellion or invasion; and then, only if the public safety demands it." In common legal practice, habeas corpus is invoked in cases where someone believes they have been wrongly detained. This applies to both people in prisons and people who are in mental institutions.

Juries

The Indiana Constitution guarantees the right of trial by jury. A jury of six (unless the parties agree to a lesser number) is called for on any civil action that requests a jury. A unanimous verdict must be reached unless a lesser state majority is agreed upon before the trial. In criminal cases, misdemeanors also have a jury of six, requiring a unanimous vote from all six. Murder or felony cases punishable by imprisonment in a state prison, have a jury of 12, all which must agree on the verdict. Jurors are chosen from a list of registered voters and may be rejected after being questioned by the attorneys and the judge in the case.

Visiting a Court

While all details of the state court system are complex, you can learn a lot about your state court system by visiting a local court. A circuit court is not far from your home and probably has hours that would allow you to watch the proceedings of some of the cases that come before it.

QUESTIONS

MULTIPLE CHOICE- Circle the letter of the correct answer.

1. Which of the following is NOT a state court?
   a. U.S. District Court   c. Supreme Court
   b. Courts of Appeals   d. County Courts
2. What are responsibilities of the IN Supreme Court?
   a. supervise lower courts   c. interpret state laws
   b. monitor court workload   d. all of the above
3. How are judges usually selected?
   a. by the governor   c. by General Assembly
   b. by the people   d. by the president
4. Which court would most likely handle a traffic ticket?:
   a. Probate Court   c. County Courts
   b. Court of Appeals   d. Supreme Court
5. Which court would rule on a death penalty case?
   a. Probate Court   c. County Courts
   b. Court of Appeals   d. Supreme Court
6. Which court is the chief trial court of the state?
   a. Circuit Court   c. County Courts
   b. Court of Appeals   d. Supreme Court

VOCABULARY MATCH - Match the statement in *Section A* with the vocabulary word in *Section B*.

A

____ 1. A lesser crime.

____ 2. Formal decisions from a court.

____ 3. The power and authority of a court.

____ 4. A more serious crime.

____ 5. The legal procedure that keeps the government from holding you indefinitely without showing cause.

B

a. opinions   b. felony   c. misdemeanor

d. habeas corpus   e. jurisdiction

INDIANA JUDICIAL BRANCH BY THE NUMBERS.
Choose the correct number from the bank that matches the statement.

Number Bank: 3, 5, 6, 7, 10, 75, 88, 90

____ Number of judicial circuits

____ Typcial number of Indiana Supreme Court justices

____ Retirement age for Supreme Court justices

____ Article number mentioning the judical system

____ Term (in years) of an IN Supreme Court justice

In a democracy, a citizen is responsible for the government under which he or she lives. By voting and staying informed on the issues, he or she participates in the business of government. With every freedom we enjoy, there are also corresponding duties. We must perform these duties, such as voting if we expect to enjoy our freedom.

Voting is a constitutional right. Early in American history, only white men over the age of 21 could vote. Then it took two constitutional amendments, one in 1870 and the other in 1920, to give Black people and women the right to vote. Then, when Americans 18 and older were in the military fighting in wars, people began to think that if young people were old enough to die for their country, they were indeed old enough to vote. In 1971, the 26th Amendment to the U.S. Constitution gave 18-year-olds the right to vote, and so did the state of Indiana.

There are three basic types of elections in Indiana. The first type is the election of representatives to operate the government. These representatives will be elected during the primary and general elections described below. The second type of election is voting on constitutional amendments (discussed previously). And the third type is the election in which the people are asked to vote on a public issue (referendum). One example of a referendum is the local school district requesting a tax increase to fund a new school.

Primary Elections

Primaries are elections held before the general election to elect one candidate from a specific political party (usually Republican or Democratic) to represent that party in the general election. *Partisan* means running with an established political party. While there are many political parties in Indiana, the two dominant parties are the Democratic and Republican parties. *Nonpartisan* means having no party affiliation.

Voting at Age 17

Indiana and 19 other states allow 17-year-olds to vote in primaries if 18 by the November election. This group is allowed to vote in primaries for federal and statewide offices. Advocates say the change allows youth to develop voting habits early, a key to ensuring they turn into lifelong voters. Critics have questioned whether teens are engaged enough to cast meaningful votes. What do you think?

The winners of these primaries then face each other in the upcoming general election. Indiana's primary election, also known as *primary election day*, is listed as a state holiday in which state government offices in Indiana are closed. It is the first Tuesday after the first Monday of May and every two years after that.

General Elections

The most publicized elections in Indiana are the *general elections*. They are *biennial* elections. That is, they are held every two years in even-numbered years.

The Indiana gubernatorial election is held every four years. and coincides with the presidential election. The next presidential election will be in 2024 (then 2028). President Biden will be eligible to run, as he will have served only one term of the maximum two terms.

Indiana is one of three states with the broadest Election Day holiday policies. The state recognizes primary and general elections for municipal, statewide, and federal offices as legal holidays. Experts have said that the United States has a low voter turnout because elections are held on a work day, imposing a significant burden on students and hourly workers who cannot take time off to vote.

Voting Options in Indiana

There are three voting options in Indiana:

1. *Absentee voting by mail:* Absentee voting is available if you meet any of the set criteria. The last day to request an absentee ballot is 12 days before the election. You can return your absentee ballot request form through the mail, in person at your local elections office, or online. Voted ballots must be received by noon on Election Day to be counted.

2. *Early In-Person voting*: Early Voting, also known as *absentee-in-person*, is available to all registered voters. Those who want to vote in person but cannot make it to the polls on Election Day may vote early. Beginning 28 days before Election Day, each county will offer locations where you can vote. A valid photo ID is required to vote early in-person.

3. *Vote on Election Day:* Anyone registered to vote in Indiana can vote at their assigned polling location between 6:00 a.m. and 6:00 p.m on Election Day. You will need to provide one of the acceptable forms of identification.

A *provisional ballot* is a ballot that is marked but is not counted at the time it is cast. It is issued to voters who cannot provide the poll workers with documentation as required by Indiana law. If you cast a provisional ballot, you will have ten days after the election to present the needed documentation or a proper form of photo ID.

Voting Requirements

In Indiana, like any state, a citizen must obey the election laws. They also must meet the requirements that have been set up by those laws. You can vote if you are:

- you are both a U.S. citizen and a resident of Indiana
- at least 18 years old on Election Day for general elections (see note regarding voting at age 17)
- registered to vote
- a resident of your election district (precinct) for at least 30 days before the election
- not in prison convicted of a crime
- not claiming the right to vote in another state
- must present a government-issued photo identification before casting a ballot at the polls

Upcoming Elections in Indiana

Upcoming General Elections: 2022, 2024 (will include gubernatorial election), 2026

Upcoming Presidential Elections: 2024, 2028

General elections are always held on the Tuesday following the first Monday of November in even-numbered years.

Political Parties

A discussion of our system of government would not be complete without a discussion of political parties. While the Founding Fathers did not plan political parties and they are not mentioned in the Constitution, political parties are a vital part of our governmental system. Political parties developed quite early in our history, even as the debate raged over whether or not to adopt the Constitution. The *Federalists* and the *Anti-Federalists* were the two groups that represented the beginning of our political parties.

Politics often has a bad reputation. An expression like "dirty politics" indicates how some people feel about the subject. Contributing to this feeling are the frequent news stories about corrupt and dishonest political figures. Citizens are responsible for the quality of politics, and it's necessary for citizens to be involved in the political system to ensure that the quality remains high.

Voter Turnout

The chart below shows the voter turnout in the United States and shows the fluctuations in presidential and midterm elections. In recent elections, leading up to the 2020 election, about 60 percent of the voting-eligible population participated in presidential elections, and about 40 percent voted during midterm elections. The 2020 election turnout of 66.2 percent set a record, with the highest turnout in 120 years. Turnout is lower for odd-year, primary, and local elections.

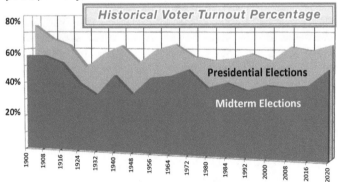

Historical Voter Turnout Percentage

Voter turnout can vary considerably from one state to the next. Minnesota had the highest voter turnout in the 2020 presidential election, with 76.9 percent of the state's voting-eligible population casting a ballot. In the 2016 presidential election, 58 percent of registered Indiana voters cast ballots. In 2020, 65 percent of registered Indiana voters made their voices heard at the polls. With the pandemic wreaking havoc across the state, many voters opted to vote absentee, which requires them to have a reason to cast a ballot by mail. Sixty-one percent of votes were absentee, compared to 33 percent in the 2016 general election.

There also are striking disparities in participation among different demographic groups. For example, the turnout rate among people ages 60 and over was about 70 percent, compared to a little over 40 percent among 18- to 29-year-olds.

The United States has historically trailed most developed countries when it comes to getting people to cast a ballot for their elected officials. The record-breaking turnout in 2020 reaffirmed that voting is a right Americans are no longer taking for granted.

Are Elections Secure in Indiana?

Voter fraud is extremely rare, both in Indiana and the United States. Misinformation can undermine public confidence in the electoral process, as well as in our democracy. Indiana takes many actions and promotes the security of the election processes. Visit the Indiana secretary of state's website (in.gov/sos) for more details.

QUESTIONS

FILL IN THE BLANKS / SHORT ANSWER

1. When is the next presidential election? _____
2. When is the next gubernatorial election? _____
3. If you are going to be absent on Election Day, how can you still vote?_____
_____
4. What is the purpose of a primary election? _____
_____

TRUE OR FALSE? Write a *T* or *F* in the space provided.

_____ 1. You must be at least 18 years old to vote in general elections.
_____ 2. A person serving a jail sentence temporarily loses the right to vote.
_____ 3. Presidential elections have the largest turnout.
_____ 4. General elections are only held when the president is being elected.
_____ 5. Election Day is always held on a Thursday.
_____ 6. You are allowed to vote in two different states.
_____ 7. The 26th Amendment changed the voting age to 18 years old.
_____ 8. Non-citizens can vote in every election.
_____ 9. Indiana has a similar voter turnout as Minnesota.

EXPRESS YOUR OPINION

Review the voter turnout data in this unit. Do you feel that the current voter participation is acceptable? When you meet the age requirement to vote, will you and why?

_____

_____

_____

It is important to remember that local government units are created at the request or with the residents' consent to provide the necessary services. Under the state constitution, the state Legislature may give local government increased or decreased powers and duties. In order to carry out these functions, the state grants them special powers, including taxing and borrowing money.

Since the 10th Amendment to the United States Constitution makes local government, for the most part, a matter of state rather than federal law, the states are free to adopt a wide variety of local government systems. There are several levels of local government in Indiana: counties, municipalities (cities and villages), townships, and special districts.

Municipal governments in Indiana are designated cities and towns. Cities are further divided into three classes as follows: (1) first-class–600,000 people or more, (2) second-class--35,000 to 599,999 people, and (3) third-class--fewer than 35,000 people. The state's local government system includes 117 cities and 456 incorporated towns. Also, a few communities that have never been incorporated into a town are governed by the board of commissioners of the county in which they are located. The largest municipality and the only first-class city in the state is Indianapolis, with more than 860,000 residents. The smallest municipalities may have as few as 200 people.

Each municipality may organize its government under certain basic forms. Among these in Indiana are the *mayor-council* and *city-manager* forms.

Mayor-Council Form

Mayor-council governments feature an elected executive officer called a *mayor* and an elected legislative body known as the *city council*. The mayor and city council work together to balance and pass a budget, draft and enforce legislation, and oversee city departments.

The mayor is the chief executive officer, and he or she enforces all laws and appoints some city officers with council approval. The mayor presides over council meetings and may vote in cases of a tie. He or she may veto the measures from the council, but that board can override the mayor's veto by a two-thirds vote. Almost all terms of office under this form are elected to four years. A *city clerk* and *treasurer* are elected officials in the executive branch.

The city council (also referred to as the common council) is the legislative and fiscal body of the city government. The council's members are made up of representatives from each of the city's districts. Members are elected officials who serve for four-year terms. The council is responsible for passing or changing local laws (known as *ordinances*), resolutions, and motions for the city's government. As the fiscal body, the council has the authority to levy certain taxes and is responsible for adopting a budget each year. The council also appoints members to specific boards and commissions that serve the community in various areas.

There are two types of mayor-council government, the *weak mayor* system and the *strong mayor* system.

1. Weak Mayor System. This system is usually found in smaller cities. This is not saying anything personal about the mayor; instead, it simply means that most of the city's power is kept with the city council. Indiana is considered a "strong mayor" state so this form is rarely used.

2. Strong Mayor System. This system is found in most cities in the state. In this type of local government, a significant amount of power is given to the mayor, although the council has power, too. The mayor is directly responsible for the city's business affairs and appoints many key officials.

City-Manager Form

The city-manager form of government, referred to as the council-manager form, may be used by the third-class cities in Indiana. The basic idea of the city-manager form is that a professionally trained manager, often an outsider, is hired by the elected city council to manage all city affairs. A mayor, elected by the people or selected by the council, presides at council meetings but seldom has greater power than council members. Most councils have from five to 10 members and are the chief governing body of the city, making laws and passing ordinances. The manager's duties include enforcing these laws, appointing department heads, and managing city services.

Counties

There are 92 counties in Indiana. All counties carry out a state policy of a general nature: they enforce laws, prosecute offenders, build and maintain roads, keep records, conduct elections, and assess and collect property taxes. In addition, counties are authorized to provide a variety of local government services, such as public health and planning, licensing, regulating land use, and establishing such diverse functions as health care, hospitals, parks, and libraries. Every county has a governing body known as the *county board*. Other officers include a sheriff, clerk, and treasurer. A coroner, recorder, assessor, auditor, and others can be appointed or elected, depending on the particular county.

Townships

The counties are divided into townships. There are 1,008 townships in Indiana, and the number per county ranges from four to 21. Like the county, the township has specific powers and is subject to state restrictions and supervision.

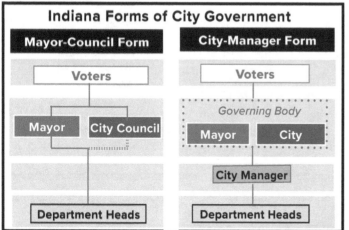

Indiana Forms of City Government

Mayor-Council Form	City-Manager Form
Voters	Voters
Mayor City Council	Governing Body: Mayor City
	City Manager
Department Heads	Department Heads

Elected officials administer township affairs, including a supervisor, clerk, assessor, and trustees. The three primary functions of township government include (1) construction and maintenance of rural roads and bridges, (2) general assistance to the needy, and (3) assessment of the property. There are also miscellaneous functions, such as voter registration, cemeteries, and mental health facilities.

Special-Purpose Districts

Various special-purpose districts have been created to provide special services for the people of Indiana. An example of a special-purpose district is the public school district. Other widespread special-purpose districts would be forest preserves, transit authorities, library districts, mosquito abatement districts, and park districts.

Principle of Home Rule

Home rule grants cities, municipalities, and counties the ability to pass laws to govern themselves as they see fit (so long as they obey the state and federal constitutions). The principle is modeled on *federalism*, giving local leaders more choice, options, flexibility, and freedom. Home rule powers in Indiana derive mostly from *The Home Rule Act of 1980*. However, local governments in Indiana are prohibited from engaging in a wide variety of activities unless the state legislature affirmatively votes to allow them, such as the powers to impose taxes, licenses, or fees, to conduct elections, and invest money.

Population Changes in Indiana

Population growth in Indiana continues to be driven by a handful of metropolitan areas. Foremost among these is the 11-county Indianapolis-Carmel-Anderson metro area, which added roughly 13,100 residents last year, accounting for 64 percent of Indiana's net growth in 2021. The Indy metro area is home to nearly 2.13 million people, representing 31 percent of the state's population and the nation's 33rd-largest metro area.

Indiana's fastest-growing counties continue to be suburban communities in the Indianapolis metro area. Boone County led the way with a 2.6 percent population gain in 2021, followed by Hamilton (2.2) and Hendricks (2.2) counties. The fastest-growing counties outside the Indianapolis area were Parke (1.6 percent growth) and Clarke (1.2). In terms of the most significant numeric gains, Hamilton County once again set the standard in 2021 by adding 7,782 residents.

QUESTIONS

TRUE OR FALSE? Write a *T* or *F* in the space provided.

___ 1. A weak mayor system is found in all Indiana cities.

___ 2. In the city-manager form, a manager runs the city.

___ 3. The mayor is the chief legislative official of the city.

___ 4. Every county has a township.

___ 5. Mayors are appointed by the governor to 3-year terms.

___ 6. A mayor does not have the power to veto legislation.

___ 7. There are 92 counties in Indiana.

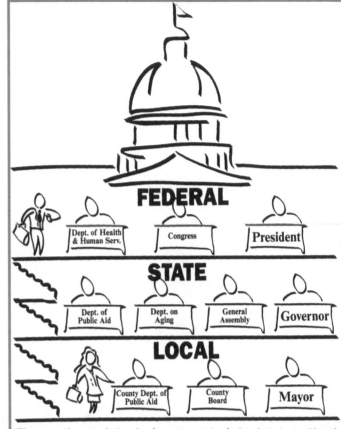

There are three main levels of government— federal, state, and local. Often the three must coordinate what they offer to you. For example, the federal Department of Human Services might provide funding for a health program. Then, the state Department of Public Aid makes sure that the program gets to the county level, and then to you.

___ 8. Special districts are created by the federal government.

___ 9. Counties follow and take direction from state government.

___ 10. A school district is a special-purpose district.

WHICH FORM OF GOVERNMENT? Which form fits the statement given? Answer *Mayor-Council (MC)*, *City-Manager (CM)*. both (*B*), or neither (*N*).

_____ 1. The mayor is responsible for the city's operation.

_____ 2. A trained manager is elected by the city council to manage city affairs.

_____ 3. The mayor presides over council meetings.

_____ 4. The governing body is the judicial branch.

_____ 5. Have a "strong" and "weak" form.

_____ 6. The principle of home rule may apply.

_____ 7. May be used by third-class cities.

SHORT ANSWER

1. Explain *home rule*. _____

_____

2. In which county do you reside? _____

3. Name one county service that directly affects you.

_____

Any discussion of government must take into account the critical problem of financing the cost of government. In recent years, government expenditures often increased faster than government revenues. Citizens demand services from their governments, and these services must be paid. Governments raise money for expenses through taxation.

Before you start the study of government taxation and finance, you need to become familiar with some commonly used terms:

revenue: _money received._ It can be considered your income or as mentioned here, the income of state governments. Your income is how much money you make. The state's income is how much it gets from taxes and other sources.

expenditure: _money paid out or spent._ Your expenditures are what you spend on groceries, clothes, cell phone, etc. Expenditures for states is how they spend their revenue.

Over $1 trillion is spent by state and local governments in our country each year. The pie chart below shows how the tax money is collected and spent in the state of Indiana each year. Indiana has a total operating budget of $46 billion per year. Today's state and local governments provide such services as public schools, welfare, police, public transportation, health programs, courts, and highway construction. The money to pay for these services comes mainly from taxes, but there are other sources.

Limitations on State Taxation

The state's taxation power is limited by the federal Constitution, the state's own laws, and its own constitution. The federal Constitution, for instance, does not allow states to make import or export taxes, nor are states allowed to tax commerce between states. The U.S. Constitution prohibits states from taxing federal property, such as military bases. Also, the 14th Amendment says that taxes must be administered fairly and for public purposes.

Indiana's biggest revenue source is the sales tax, followed by the state personal income tax, then business and other smaller tax sources.

Sales Taxes

Taxes on the sale of goods, called _sales taxes_, provide states with more than half of their incomes. Forty-five states, including Indiana, have a general sales tax.

Income Taxes

Forty-three states, including Indiana, tax personal income. Forty-six states make corporations pay tax on their incomes as well. Indiana has a corporate income tax also. Over one-third of states' tax revenues are provided by _income tax._

Property Taxes

The traditional source of tax money for state and local government has been the tax on _property._ While less important now on the state level, it currently provides most of the revenue for local government. The county treasurer is the property tax collector and custodian of all monies with responsibility for investing funds and maintaining an adequate cash flow.

State Budgets

1920s, they were put together in a confused manner with each state department fighting for funds. Today's budgets must be carefully drawn. The four major areas to which most state budgets give money are education, highways, public welfare, and retirement and unemployment benefits.

Although the governor, in most states, has the responsibility to make the budget, he or she usually has a professional budget director and staff. The Indiana Constitution requires the governor to prepare and submit a balanced state budget to the General Assembly. Indiana is one of 20 states that produce a budget every other year for the upcoming two fiscal years, or biennially. The enacted budget averages a total annual spending of $46 billion. Its fiscal year begins July 1. The governor presents the budget in a speech to the General Assembly in Indianapolis.

Collecting and spending such funds is indeed a tremendous responsibility for the governor and the General Assembly. If citizens want to see this money collected fairly and spent wisely, they need to be involved and informed citizens. By participating in your current studies, you are beginning to meet your responsibility.

Typical Indiana Budget - Spending

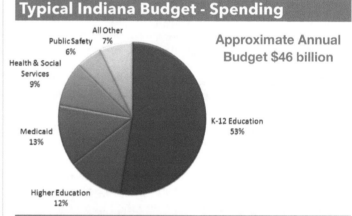

Approximate Annual Budget $46 billion

All Other 7%
Public Safety 6%
Health & Social Services 9%
Medicaid 13%
Higher Education 12%
K-12 Education 53%

QUESTIONS

FILL IN THE BLANKS

1. The annual Indiana budget is presented by the _____ .

2. The budget is presented to the _____ .

3. The fiscal year of the state begins in _____ .

4. States are not allowed to make _i_ _____ or _e_ _____ taxes.

5. Annual spending in Indiana is now $ _____ billion.

TRUE OR FALSE? Write a _T_ or _F_ in the space provided.

____ 1. The U.S. Constitution puts some limitations on state taxation.

____ 2. Indiana does not receive any money from the federal government.

____ 3. Sales taxes are a significant source of income.

____ 4. Education is the largest item in Indiana spending.

____ 5. Indiana gets very little money from income taxes.

Indiana History

I. Indiana has had two capitals since it became a state in 1816:
   A. Corydon
   B. Indianapolis
II. There have been two Indiana Constitutions:
   A. 1816
   B. 1851, currently in effect with numerous amendments
      1. Longer than, but similar to, the federal Constitution; can be changed by amendment.
      2. Provides basic form and operation of state and local government; must not conflict with the federal Constitution or with authority given to the federal government.

The Three Branches of Indiana Constitutional Government

I. There are three branches of Indiana government:
   A. *Legislative Branch*, Article 4
      1. Main duty is to make laws
      2. Main body is the General Assembly
         A. The General Assembly consists of two houses:
            1. The Senate
               a. 50 members, one from each of the 50 senatorial districts
               b. Qualifications: must be 25 years of age or older, residents of the district at least one year, and a citizen of the United States for two years.
               c. Your local state senator is _____.
               d. Term: four years, half selected every even-numbered year
               e. Powers: pass bills and send to House, try impeachments, approve governor's appointments
               f. Officers: president of the Senate, served by the lieutenant governor, president pro tempore, majority and minority leaders
            2. The House of Representatives
               a. 100 members, one from each of the 100 representative districts
               b. Qualifications: must be 21 years of age or older, residents of the district at least one year, and a citizen of the United States for two years.
               c. Your local representative is _____.
               d. Term: two years, election in even-numbered years
               e. Powers: pass bills and send to Senate, start impeachment
               f. Officers: speaker of the House, elected by members of the House of Representatives, speaker pro tempore, majority and minority leaders
         B. Lawmaking process is similar to that of the United States Congress.
         C. Salaries: $28,103 annually for members of the General Assembly.
      3. Each Indiana General Assembly exists for two years and has one session annually; extra sessions may be called by the governor.
      4. Lawmaking process: bills must pass both houses and be sent to the governor;
         A. If the governor signs, the bill is law; he or she has seven days and if no action the bill becomes law;
         B. If the governor vetoes, the General Assembly can override with majority vote, and if they do, bill is law without the governor's signature.
   B. *Executive Branch*, Article 5
      1. Main duty: enforce and administer state laws
      2. Chief executive is the Governor of Indiana
         A. Qualifications:
            1. Must be at least 30 years old
            2. Resident of the state for five years preceding the election, and a U.S. citizen
         B. Duties of the governor:
            1. Appoints many state officials
            2. Approves or vetoes bills from the General Assembly
            3. Commander-in-chief of state militia
            4. May grant pardons, commutations, and reprieves
            5. May call special sessions of the General Assembly

continued

  B. *Executive Branch*, Article 5 (continued)

    C. Governor's salary: $134,051 per year

    D. Term: Four years (limited to two consecutive terms with at least four years before the same individual may hold the office again.)

   3. Other executive branch officers

    A. The lieutenant governor assumes jobs assigned by the governor.

    B. Other executive officials elected by the voters of the state: attorney general, the secretary of state, state treasurer, and auditor.

    C. All executive officers are elected together and serve four-year terms.

  C. *Judicial Branch*, Article 7

   1. Main duty: interpret laws, administer justice

   2. The judicial power of the state is vested in a Supreme Court, a court of appeals, and circuit courts

    A. Indiana Supreme Court

      1. Original jurisdiction in some cases, final court of appeal in cases from lower courts

      2. Five judges, 10-year elected terms

    B. Court of Appeals: hears appeals from circuit courts; number fixed by law; 10-year terms for judges

    C. Circuit courts: chief trial courts, judges selected for six-year terms, 90 judicial circuits.

Voting and Elections

I. Elections

  A. *Primary elections* (held in May biennially), nominate a candidate for their party

  B. *General elections* (held in November, biennially), to select both state and national candidates

II. Voting

  A. *Requirements:* Must be 18 years of age (17-year-olds can vote in primaries if they will be 18 by the general election), must be a U.S. citizen, a registered voter, and citizen of the state for at least 30 days before election

  B. Three voting options in Indiana

   1. *absentee voting by mail*

   2. *early in-person voting*

   3. *vote on Election Day*

Local Government

I. Local governments established and organized under state constitution and state laws:

  A. Municipal government includes cities, villages, and townships

   1. Cities use mayor-and-council form of municipal government

    A. Mayor is chief executive officer and city council is legislative body

    B. City treasurer and clerk are other elected officials

   2. *Home rule* grants cities, municipalities, and/or counties the ability to pass laws to govern themselves

  B. Special-purpose districts, provide special services for the people of Indiana

  C. County government, carry out state policy

   1. 92 counties in Indiana

   2. Provide a variety of local government duties

   3. Governing body is the county board

  D. Townships, counties are divided into townships that have specific state powers

Financing Government

I. Indiana fiscal year is July 1 through June 30 (ex. FY23 is July 1, 2022, to June 30, 2023)

II. Taxes help fund state and local government services

  A. Sales taxes

  B. Income taxes

  C. Property taxes

III. State budgets are prepared and submitted annually by the governor

  A. State receives and spends approximately $46 billion annually

  B. Lawmakers and public officials are elected in part to manage the state's finances

This sheet to be filled out when you complete the Indiana section. The numbers in parentheses gives the page number where the answer or additional information may be found.

1. What cities have hosted the state capital? (54) _____ .

2. When was the first Indiana Constitution written? (55, 56) _____

   When was the present Indiana Constitution written? (55, 58) _____

3. Name the states included in the Northwest Territory. (56) _____

4. Explain how to amend the Indiana Constitution. (59) _____

   _____

   _____

5. What is the main body in the Legislative Branch? (62) _____

   What two chambers does it contain? (62) _____

6. What is the main purpose of the legislative branch? (62) _____

7. What are the qualifications for becoming a member of the Legislature? (62) _____

8. How many members in the state Senate? (62)_____ In the state House? (63)_____

9. Who is the presiding officer of the state Senate? (62) _____

10. Who is the presiding officer of the state House? (63) _____

11. Explain the lawmaking process in Indiana. (64-66) _____

    _____

    _____

12. What can the General Assembly do after a veto by the governor? (64) _____

13. What is a quorum in the General Assembly? (62) _____

14. Name one special duty of the state Senate. (62) _____

15. Name one special duty of the state House of Representatives. (62) _____

16. What helps the General Assembly conduct business efficiently in lawmaking? (64) _____

17. What are lobbies? (65) _____

18. What is the main purpose of the executive branch? (67) _____

19. What are the qualifications for governor? (67) _____

    _____

20. What is the governor's salary? (67)_____ How many years in a term? (67) _____

21. What is the order of succession to the governor's office? (67) _____

22. What is the main purpose of the judicial branch? (69) _____

23. What is the primary function of the courts of appeals? (70) _____

24. How many Indiana Supreme Court justices? (70) _____

25. Name two duties of the Indiana Supreme Court. (70) _____

26. What is a civil case? (69) _____

27. Name three requirements to vote in Indiana. (72) _____

    _____

28. Describe the options for voting if you are not available on Election Day. (72) _____

    _____

29. When is the next general election in Indiana? (72-73) _____

30. How many counties in Indiana and what is their main function? (74) _____

    _____

31. Explain a "strong mayor" system of government. (74) _____

32. What is the principle of "home rule?" (75) _____

33. Give an example of a special-purpose district. (75) _____

34. Name three taxes that Indiana residents can expect to pay. (76) _____

35. Explain the roles of the governor and Legislature in the budget process. (76) _____

    _____

The following test will help you prepare for your final state unit test. It has questions similar to ones you will find on your final. It is suggested you write your answers on a piece of paper so you can take the test a number of times. You will find the correct answers at the bottom of Page 81.

MATCHING - Which Branch of Indiana government?

Match the person or body in **Column A** with the correct branch of state government in **Column B**. Put the letter of the correct answer in the space provided.

Column A

_____ 1. The Governor
_____ 2. The House of Representatives
_____ 3. The State Supreme Court
_____ 4. Circuit Courts
_____ 5. Lieutenant Governor
_____ 6. State Senate
_____ 7. Attorney General

Column B

a. The Legislative Branch
b. The Judicial Branch
c. The Executive Branch

FILL IN THE BLANKS - Write the correct answer in the space provided.

_____   8. Who can veto a bill passed by the General Assembly?
_____   9. If the governor is unable to serve, who becomes governor?
_____   10. The next gubernatorial election in Indiana.
_____   11. The most common type of municipal government used by first and second-class cities.
_____   12. The governor of Indiana.
_____   13. The next presidential election will be in this year.
_____   14. How many days does the governor have to consider a bill from the General Assembly?
_____   15. How many constitutions has Indiana had?
_____   16. Who may call special sessions of the General Assembly?
_____   17. The chief election officer of the state.
_____   18. The chief legal officer of the state
_____   19. How are Indiana judges selected?
_____   20. Name the election used to select candidates for the general election.
_____   21. The capital of Indiana.
_____   22. If the General Assembly wishes to pass a bill over a veto, what vote is necessary?

MATCHING - Which State Court?

Match the statement in **Column A** with the correct court in **Column B**. Put the letter of the correct answer in the space provided.

_____ 23. Chief trial court of the state.
_____ 24. Would handle violations like traffic tickets
_____ 25. The highest court in Indiana
_____ 26. There is one in all 92 counties
_____ 27. Has five districts with 15 judges
_____ 28. Oversees the entire court system
_____ 29. Final authority on the state constitution

a. Supreme Court
b. Court of Appeals
c. Circuit Courts
d. County Courts

continued

MATCHING - Which Chamber of the General Assembly?

Match the statement in *Column A* with the correct chamber of the Legislature in *Column B*. Put the letter of the correct answer in the space provided.

Column A

_____ 30. Must be 25 years old or older

_____ 31. Are appointed by the governor

_____ 32. Declare laws unconstitutional

_____ 33. Have lawmaking responsibilities

_____ 34. They are elected by the people

_____ 35. Have 100 members and 100 districts

_____ 36. Have 50 members and 50 districts

_____ 37. Are parts of the General Assembly

_____ 38. Has speaker for chief officer

_____ 39. Has lieutenant governor as chief officer

_____ 40. Their term is two years

_____ 41. Their term is four years

_____ 42. Begin impeachment proceedings

_____ 43. Receives no salary

_____ 44. Makes laws for states outside of Indiana

_____ 45. They meet in Indianapolis

Column B

a. House of Representatives

b. Senate

c. Both

d. Neither

TRUE OR FALSE? - Write a *T* or *F* in the space provided.

_____ 46. Both the Indiana Constitution and the United States Constitution have bills of rights.

_____ 47. The governor is commander-in-chief of the state militia.

_____ 48. Indiana became a state in 1848 and was the 21st state.

_____ 49. Foreign affairs is one of the duties of state government.

_____ 50. Our governor must be 40 years old or older.

_____ 51. You can vote in primary elections at age 17.

_____ 52. There are 92 counties in Indiana.

_____ 53. The 10th Amendment of the U.S. Constitution recognizes the power of states.

_____ 54. The biggest item in state spending is for highways.

_____ 55. Most of the Indiana court cases would take place in the Supreme Court.

This is the end of your Indiana Constitution self-test. Please take the following steps:

1. Correct your test by using the answers below.

2. Any mistakes you have should have made should be reviewed, corrected, and studied.

3. You should take the test over, paying special attention to any previous incorrect answers.

Your number of correct answers: _____

Your number of incorrect answers: _____

Total = _____**55**_____

Answers: 1. c 2. a 3. b 4. b 5. c 6. a 7. c 8. Governor 9. Lieutenant Governor 10. 2024 (then 2028) 11. mayor-council 12. answer will vary 13. 2024 14. seven 15. two 16. Governor 17. Secretary of State 18. Attorney General 19. elected by voters 20. Primary Election 21. Indianapolis 22. majority 23. c 24. c 25. a 26. c 27. b 28. a 29. c 30. c 31. d 32. d 33. c 34. c 35. a 36. b 37. c 38. a 39. b 40. a 41. b 42. a 43. d 44. d 45. c 46. T 47. T 48. F 49. F 50. F 51. T 52. T 53. T 54. F 55. F

This glossary contains constitution-related terms to aid in the study of the federal Constitution. Many, but not all, of these terms are used in the worktext. These terms can be used to expand your knowledge of the Constitution, government, and our democracy.

act – a bill, or proposal for a law, passed by a majority of lawmakers.

adjourn – to terminate a session (of Congress, or of a court) or suspend until a later time.

ambassador – an official who represents his or her government in dealings with another nation.

amendments – changes in a bill, a law, or a constitution.

appeal – to request another trial before a higher court.

appeals court – a federal court that reviews the decision a lower (trial) court.

appoint – to name someone to fill an office.

appropriation – money set aside for a specific use by an act of the legislature.

article – a segment of a written document. The Constitution is divided into articles dealing with different areas of government.

assembly – a public meeting or gathering; also the name commonly given to the larger house in the state legislature.

attorney general – the head of the executive department who is chiefly responsible for enforcing U.S. laws or state laws.

bail – the sum of money that an accused person may deposit with a court as a security to get out of jail while awaiting trial.

bicameral legislature – a lawmaking body with two houses.

bill – a proposal for a law to be considered by Congress or a state legislature.

bill of attainder – a law naming a person guilty of a crime without trial (such are not allowed by the U.S. Constitution).

Bill of Rights – the first ten amendments of the U.S. Constitution; their common purpose is to protect the American people from abuses of government power.

budget – a plan for spending money over a certain period of time.

cabinet – a group of department heads who meet regularly with the president or with a state's governor.

campaign – an organized effort carried out over a period of months or years; specifically, the efforts of a candidate and his or hers supports to win election.

caucus – a meeting of party members to decide policy or nominate candidates.

censorship – a government's practice of stopping certain ideas from being published or expressed.

census – an official count of the U.S. population conducted every ten years.

charter – a document granting powers of self-government to a city or municipality; also a document giving legal status to a business organization.

checks and balances – a system by which each branch of government has the power to block or overrule the decisions of the other branches.

chief executive – the elected official who is chiefly responsible for enforcing the laws of a state (the governor) or a nation (the president).

circuit court – a court in the federal system that has the power to hear appeals from trial courts.

citizen – anyone who is officially counted as a member of a nation or state.

citizenship – the status of being a citizen.

civil case – a dispute brought to court for settlement.

civil rights – rights which are considered to be unquestionable, deserved be all people under all circumstances.

cloture – a means of preventing a filibuster on a bill.

commander-in-chief – the supreme commander of a nation's armed forces; in the U.S. it is the president.

commerce – business transactions, trade, or the buying and selling of goods on a large scale.

commission form – a plan of local government in which legislative and executive powers are shared by a group of elected officials known as "commissioners."

commutations – changing a prison sentence or other penalty to another less severe.

compromise – to give up a part of one's original demands or desires in order to reach agreement on an issue.

conference committee – a group of lawmakers drawn from both houses of Congress (or a state legislature) with the purpose to resolve the differences between two versions of a bill passed by the two houses.

confirmation – the process by which the U.S. Senate approves a president's appointments to office.

Congress – chief legislative body of our nation.

conservative – someone who wants government's role in society and the economy to be strictly limited; may also refer to changes in policy to be gradual, not rapid.

consideration – A proposed bill that is read to each house of the General Assembly.

constituents – the residents of a district or state who are represented by a legislator from that same district or state.

constitution – the set of basic laws and rules defining a nation's or state's system of government.

convention – a large meeting of delegates from different states or districts.

council-manager system – a system of local government in which legislative power belongs to an elected group (the council), which hires a professional manager to conduct city business.

criminal case – a matter involving the violation of a state or federal law.

debate – a formal process for presenting arguments for and against a bill or a public issue.

defendant – the person at a trial who been accused of some offense, injury, or crime.

deficit – the amount of annual debt.

delegated powers – those rights that the federal government is free to exercise because they are specifically mentioned in the Constitution.

delegates – persons to chosen to represent others at a special meeting.

democracy – a system of government in which the people (citizens and voters) have the final power.

department – a major division of the executive branch.

depression – a more serious and long slowdown in the economy.

diplomacy – the means by which nations communicate with one another and try to settle their differences peacefully.

discrimination – the practice of favoring one person or one group over another.

district courts – federal courts that hold trials.

domestic policy – government's decisions about issues within the nation.

double jeopardy – the putting of an accused person on trial a second time after that person has been found innocent in the first trial (prohibited by the Constitution).

elastic clause – a statement in the Constitution giving Congress the power to do what is "necessary and proper" for carrying out its other powers.

Electoral College – the group of politicians (several from each state) who are authorized by the Constitution to cast official ballots for president and vice president.

embargo – agreement prohibiting (not allowing) trade.

excise tax – a tax on the sale of specific items, such as gasoline.

executive branch – the part of the U.S. government headed by the president and responsible for enforcing federal laws.

executive power – the ability of an official or group of officials to enforce and carry out the laws.

export – to ship (commodities) to other countries or places for sale, exchange, etc.

ex post facto law – a law that would punish acts committed in the past, though they had been legal at the time (prohibited by the Constitution).

expressed powers – powers actually mentioned or expressed in the Constitution (also called enumerated powers).

extradition – the process by which a criminal is returned to the state where the crime was committed.

federal government – the United States government.

federalism – a political system that gives significant powers to both national and state governments.

felony – a serious crime usually punished by a jail sentence.

filibuster – a tactic of making long speeches on the Senate floor as a means of defeating a bill.

fiscal policy – the government's taxing and spending policies.

fiscal year – the U.S. federal government's fiscal year is the 12-month period beginning on October 1st and ending on September 30th.

foreign policy – one government's goals and methods in dealing with foreign governments.

full faith and credit clause – a clause in the U.S. Constitution which says that every state must recognize and respect the laws and judgments of other states.

general assembly – the name of a state legislature comprising of the state House of Representatives and the state Senate.

general election – an election usually held at regular intervals in which candidates are elected in all or most constituencies of a nation or state.

gerrymandering – drawing the boundaries of a voting district so that the political party in power has an advantage over rival parties.

government – a system for managing a community or nation and the leaders or lawmakers who control that system.

grand jury – a group of citizens who decide where there is enough evidence to indict (accuse) a person of a crime.

grievance – a cause of complaint.

habeas corpus – an arrested person's right to appear before a judge. If the judge finds no legal reason to detain the person, he or she must be released.

home rule – the privilege granted to some communities to decide how their local governments will be organized.

immigration – the movement of people of foreign birth from their own country to an adopted country.

impeachment – to accuse an official of wrong doing. This step precedes trial and removal from office.

implied powers – powers that are not actually expressed but believed to be a power of the Congress.

inauguration – a ceremony for beginning the term of office of a president, a vice president, or some other official.

income tax – a tax collected on wages, salaries, tips, and other forms of personal earnings.

incorporate – to form legally a business or community that has received a special charter from the state.

indict – to formally accuse a person suspected of committing a crime.

initiative – a procedure by which voters may propose a law without going through the legislature.

interest group – people with a common political goal who try to persuade government to pass laws implementing their ideas.

interstate commerce – trade or business transactions carried out across state lines.

judicial branch – the part of government made up of courts, with its function to interpret laws in specific cases.

judicial power – the ability of judges to decide court cases based upon the interpretation of the laws and the Constitution.

judicial review – the power of a federal court, especially the Supreme Court, to determine whether the acts of Congress and the president are allowed by the Constitution.

judiciary – the court system.

jurisdiction – a court's authority to decide certain kinds of cases and not others.

justice – the ideal of settling disputes and determining responsibility for crime in a fair manner.

left – a reference to people who have liberal ideas.

legislative branch – the part of government that has responsibility for making the laws.

legislative power – the ability of certain officials to make laws for a city, a state, or a nation.

legislator – a member of a lawmaking body.

legislature – a group of elected officials who make the laws.

liberal – someone who thinks government should take an active role in promoting social and economic progress. Also, someone who favors rapid change.

liberty – the right to make free choices and to express opinions without fear of being arrested and punished.

libel – any spoken or written statement which defames a person or exposes him or her to public contempt or ridicule.

lobbies – organized efforts by interest groups to influence the opinion and votes of lawmakers.

lobbyist – a person hired by an interest group to speak to legislators about bills that concern the group.

logrolling – an informal agreement between lawmakers that they will vote for the bill that each is most interested in.

lower house – the chamber in a two-house legislature that has more members than the other.

majority – part of a group that is more than half the total.

majority leader – someone chosen by members of the majority party to lead their lawmaking efforts. The majority party is the one holding the most seats in the legislature.

mayor-and-council form – a plan of city government in which the executive is an elected mayor and the legislature is an elected body of councilors or aldermen/women.

minority leader – someone chosen by members of the minority party to lead their lawmaking efforts. The minority party is the one that holds fewer than half the seats in the legislature.

misdemeanor – a minor violation of the law that is punishable by a fine or short jail sentence.

moderate – someone whose political opinions fall in between those a liberal on the one hand and a conservative on the other.

municipality – any city or town that the state permits to be self-governing.

national debt – the total sum of money owed by the federal government.

naturalization – the process by which an immigrant to the United States may become a citizen.

nominate – to name someone as a candidate for office; to select a party member to be the party's candidate for election.

ordinance – a law passed by a local government.

original jurisdiction – the authority possessed by a court to hear and decide a case first, not an appeal from another court.

override – the ability of Congress or a state legislature to pass a bill a second time after the executive vetoes (or rejects) it.

pardon – a decision of the governor or the president to stop criminal proceedings against an accused person or to free a prisoner.

petit jury – a group of citizens, usually 12 in number, who reach a verdict (decision) at a trial after listening to the evidence.

pigeonhole – to kill a bill in committee by laying it aside and never considering it.

plaintiff – the person at a trial who claims to have been injured in some way.

platform – a political party's declaration of what it stands for on a number of issues.

pocket signature rule – if the governor does not act, the bill will automatically become law.

pocket veto – a president's way of defeating an act of Congress by taking no action on it until Congress adjourns. This method can be used only within the last ten days that Congress is in session.

political action committee (PAC) – an organization formed by a group of citizens to raise money for a candidate's campaign.

political party – an organization whose members help one another to win elections and shape government policy.

polling place – a building where people come to vote on Election Day.

popular sovereignty – the principle that the power to govern belongs to the people (either directly or through representation).

popular vote – vote of all the people participating in an election.

pork barrel projects – construction projects authorized by Congress that involves spending federal money in local areas.

preamble - the first paragraph of the Constitution.

president pro tempore - an officer of the Senate who presides when the vice president is absent.

primary – an election by members to determine who will be the candidates of the party.

progressive tax – any tax that takes more from high income people than from low-income people.

prohibit – a law, order, or decree that forbids something.

property tax – a tax collected by local government on the value of lands, buildings, and major articles of property.

prosecutor – an attorney employed by the state to prove in court that an accused person is guilty of a certain crime.

qualifications – conditions that a person must meet in order to hold a government office or to exercise some privilege such as voting.

quorum – number of legislators that must be present in a chamber in order to conduct official business.

ratification – act of approving or making legal.

reapportionment – the changing of the boundaries of voting districts in order to allow for changes in population.

recall – a special election to decide whether or not a state official is to be removed from office.

recession – a slowdown in the economy.

redistricting – the redrawing of congressional boundaries.

referendum – an election on a proposed law that voters (not legislators) can either adopt or reject.

regressive tax – any tax that takes proportionately more from low-income people rather than from high-income people.

representative government – government run by elected representatives of the people.

reprieves - delays of punishment.

reserved powers – the powers belonging to a state government.

revenues – taxes and other money received by government as income.

segregation – a practice (now illegal) of providing separate schools and other public facilities based upon your race.

separation of powers – the division of a government into three main parts or branches.

session – the period of time during which a legislature is meeting.

sovereign – the power of a completely independent nation to run its own affairs.

speaker of the house – the presiding officer of the U.S. House of Representatives or of the lower house of a state legislature.

standing committee – a committee (group of lawmakers) that continues to work from one term of the legislature to the next.

succession - order of replacement.

suffrage – voting rights.

summons – an order to appear in court.

surplus – when the government receives more money than it spends for a particular year.

tariff – a tax on imports (foreign goods) as they enter a country.

tax – money required of citizens of a nation to meet the cost of government operations.

treason – the crime of betraying one's country.

treaty – a written agreement between the governments of two or more nations.

trial – formal process in a court for determining the innocence or guilt of a person.

trustee village form – a form of local government run by trustees and a village president.

unalienable – not to be given or taken away.

unconstitutional – not allowed by the Constitution.

unicameral legislature – a lawmaking body with only one house.

union – combining of individual states into one nation.

upper house – the chamber in a two-house legislature that has fewer members than the other.

verdict – a jury's decision at the end of a trial.

veto – a chief executive's decision to reject an act of the legislature.

whip – a legislative leader who tries to persuade members of his or her party to vote a certain way on a bill.